HO'OPONOPONO

YOUR PATH TO TRUE FORGIVENESS

DR. MATT JAMES

Ho'oponopono: Your Path to True Forgiveness
By Dr. Matt James

Copyright © 2017 by Dr. Matt James

Crescendo Publishing, LLC
300 Carlsbad Village Drive
Ste. 108A, #443
Carlsbad, California 92008-2999
GetPublished@CrescendoPublishing.com
1-877-575-8814

ISBN: 978-1-944177-79-9 (p)
ISBN: 978-1-944177-80-5 (e)

Printed in the United States of America

10 9 8 7 6 5 4 3 2 1

A Message from the Author

https://youtu.be/G9GUqytopQ0

Download your complimentary seven-minute
Ho'oponopono Guided Induction from our membership
site www.empowermentsuccess.com

Introduction

I don't know why you're reading this book, but I can tell you why I wrote this book:

Ho'oponopono saved my daughter's life.

The process I want to share with you is very near and dear to my heart. It's from the twenty-eighth-generation lineage of Huna that I am privileged to carry on. "Huna" is a modern label for an ancient practice of energy work, empowerment, and flexibility of the spirit, mind, and body. The more appropriate label is "Ho'omana," which means "empowerment." A process that is fundamental to this practice and to the Hawaiian culture is ho'oponopono.

Twenty-eight generations of this lineage taught and practiced ho'oponopono before me; I've been teaching Huna and ho'oponopono since the late 1990s, and now my son is teaching it.

I teach many powerful techniques and practices, yet because ho'oponopono saved my daughter's life, I could dedicate the rest of my life to teaching and sharing it with people for that reason alone.

It all happened when my daughter, Skylar, was five and in kindergarten. Through a long series of events, I had become chairman of the board of the school that she and my son attended, working with some amazing teachers and counselors.

Early one Saturday morning, my cell phone rang, and it was the lady who handled enrollment and some of the counseling issues for the school. I knew the teachers and staff had gone out celebrating the night before, so I teased her by saying, "I'm surprised you're up so early." When I heard her tone, however, I immediately switched gears. Something was clearly wrong.

She said, "I'm calling you for two reasons. The first is because you're chairman of the board and also because you are a doctor of psychology. I thought you could help with this situation." She paused and took a deep breath. "We lost a student this weekend. I was just informed that one of our students passed away, and we're going to need help with the grieving process." She took another deep breath, and I took one with her.

She continued. "I need your help and the help of the board to handle the situation. We're just not equipped to deal with something like this." It was a small school, about 120 kids total. I immediately started jotting down notes, knowing who I needed to talk to, figuring out the task force we'd need to create. I talked with her about what we'd need to do from a logistics standpoint.

When I felt I had the ball sufficiently rolling on that front, I said, "Okay, you said you called me for two reason. What's the second one?"

She hesitated and said, "We're asking the parents to inform their kids because, again, we're not equipped to deal with having to share this information with the kids."

I said, "Sure, I understand." Her voice was shaky as she continued. "The name of the student that passed away

Table of Contents

Dedication

This book is dedicated to my daughter, Skylar. From the moment I held you, I knew you were the perfect daughter for me. You have been a gift in my life, you have softened my heart, and you have helped me become a better man. Skylar, you have the biggest heart and you are the most caring person I know. All the love and beauty you carry is in total harmony with the strength you have within. I treasure our amazing connection and I look forward to watching you grow into an empowered woman.

is Carmen." My heart sank. The school had two students named Carmen: an older boy and a kindergartener who was Skylar's best friend. "Do you know who your daughter's best friend is?"

"Yes," I whispered.

"Okay," she said. "Then you know that Carmen had leukemia. I was just informed by her parents that she passed away this morning."

My body and mind wanted to go into shock, but I continued to listen. "Matt, the situation is a lot worse than just that." She said, "Skylar took Carmen to the nurse's office on Friday because she wasn't feeling well after eating lunch. She sat there and held Carmen's hand and said, 'Don't worry. Your mommy will come pick you up. She'll make you feel better. And I'll see you on Monday. Everything will be fine.' She kept repeating those things over and over again while holding her hand."

At that point, I began to cry because I knew this news would break my daughter's big, beautiful heart. I understood why the school needed me to tell her. I prepared myself, then I sat Skylar down.

If you're a parent, I pray you never have to see your child completely lose it spiritually, mentally, emotionally, and physically. Despite all the tools I have and the decades I've been teaching, my feeling of helplessness was overwhelming.

My little five-year-old sat there hyperventilating and crying, saying over and over, "I don't understand. What do you mean—I'm never going to see my best friend again?" She couldn't comprehend what death is or why this would happen. Facing her despair was one of the most difficult moments in my life. She asked, "Why would God do this?"

How do you answer that?

Skylar didn't sleep. She went to school where it got even worse. A couple of her other friends started having eating issues, Skylar began to develop an eating issue too. Leukemia took her best friend's life, yet these five-year-old minds remembered that Carmen ate lunch, didn't feel good, and never came back. So all of a sudden, we had three five-year-olds, all of whom are really good friends, with sleeping and eating issues. To say it was tough is an understatement.

A few weeks later, Skylar was eating breakfast and just began to lose it, crying hysterically. My son, Ethan, slid across the bench and put his arm around her. He held her while she cried, then said to her very gently, "Why aren't you asking Dad for help?"

"What can Dad do?" she sobbed.

And he said, "Well, Dad helped me. I had a lot of fear when I was your age." He shared with her his first experience of doing an Introduction to Huna workshop with me, where we were doing energy and release work.

I had forgotten about this, but during that workshop, Ethan released a huge amount of fear. We were riding up the elevator afterwards, and he looked at me and said, "Dad, what you do is magic."

He was about ten at the time. I remember smiling and asking, "What do you mean, 'It was magic'?"

Ethan shrugged and said, "I don't have any fear anymore."

"Fear of what?"

He grinned and said, "Elevators." I had forgotten that Ethan had been trapped in an elevator during an earthquake years before. He said, "My heart isn't racing. I feel fine. Dad, what you do is magic."

We got up to our hotel room and sat down on the beds. Ethan looked across at me and said, "I want to test the big one." I nodded. I knew what he meant. Ever since he was a kid, Ethan never wanted to talk about death or anyone dying or anything dying. He would burst into tears and leave the room.

That was weird for me because, growing up with my grandfather, we talked about death a lot—there was no big issue with it. My grandfather said to me one time, "Hey, Matt, I'm not going to be here one day. What do you want?"

I said, "I want your desk."

And my grandfather said, "Okay, well, it's yours. But not yet. You got to wait." As I'm writing this book, I'm sitting at a desk that was my grandfather's. My grandfather and I just talked about death like it was a part of life.

Ethan couldn't. But that day he said, "Dad, I want to test the big one."

I smiled and said, "Go for it."

He shut his eyes and opened them a minute later. "Dad, it's gone. I'm totally okay if you die." He paused, then immediately backpedaled, saying, "Well, I don't want you to die. I'd be sad. But I'd get over it, and I would be okay." Next, he started to apologize, but I interrupted.

"Ethan, just stop. It's okay." It was gone. His fear of death and dying was gone. He shared this with Skylar that morning, and she laughed a little.

Skylar gave me a shaky smile and said, "Daddy, can you tell me what ho'oponopono is? Please explain this to me."

I did. And I shared with her why to do it, and what to do, and how to do it. Part of the process involves disconnecting with the person who is the focus of the process; Skylar said she wasn't ready for that yet, so I gave her time.

About two or three days later, she came up to me after school, and she said, "Okay, Daddy, I want to do it." I took her through the process.

The first time through, there was an immediate shift in the depth of her grieving. It wasn't all gone; Skylar still felt a little bit of sadness, which is perfectly natural, yet she slept that night, and she began eating better. Like peeling back layers of an onion, we did ho'oponopono a few more times. Eventually, things got back to normal. Skylar was able to talk about Carmen and about the experience without crying. She began to express her emotions in a very calm, centered way.

The healing process continued for Skylar. I asked to share the technique with the parents who were open to it. Unfortunately, some parents weren't open. Though their child was suffering the trauma of losing a friend, they didn't believe in "that energy stuff."

Last year, we were on our annual vacation in Italy, and Skylar was nine. We have a family tradition of toasting at dinner, so I asked Skylar, "What are we going to toast tonight?"

She said, "I would like to do a toast to Carmen."

Ethan asked, "What do you want to say about Carmen?"

Skylar sat up and grinned. "By now, she's probably in a new body and maybe even beginning to go to school. I hope that she has friends that love her as much as I did, and that this time, she gets to stick around a lot longer. I'm very thankful that I got to have the time that I had with her."

Ethan gave her a big hug, and I started crying. Skylar looked at me, confused. "Daddy, are you okay? Do you need to do hoʻoponopono now?"

Did hoʻoponopono literally save my daughter's life?

Today, one of Skylar's friends whom we see every once in a while will exercise after eating a salad for dinner. She'll eat a few bites of food then immediately drop down on the ground to do sit-ups and push-ups. At the age of nine, this young girl has developed an eating disorder. I believe it is directly linked to Carmen's death and the girl's unconscious (or conscious) belief that Carmen died because of something she ate.

In contrast, I have my daughter, who has healed beautifully from the trauma of the experience of losing her best friend.

We're all given a choice. It doesn't matter if you're five, if you're nine, or if you're fifty-nine—you have a choice.

You have a choice regarding how you experience the things you experience in your life. Losing someone special to you hurts. I've lost teachers and spiritual guides, and I've lost grandparents. I'd never claim that losing someone is easy.

Ho'oponopono is often called the "forgiveness practice." It is a forgiveness process, but it is also a release process. Having grown up in Hawai'i, I was taught by various elders that you need to become *pono* (*pono* means to be right with yourself, and centered) again after losing someone, that you need to free yourself from any baggage connected to them and allow that person to live on in your memories. When this happens, you can heal inside.

I will tell you inspiring stories of my students and people I've taught to become teachers who have experienced a total transformation in their lives after experiencing ho'oponopono and adopting it as a regular practice. It is not the only tool I have in my arsenal, but when it comes to releasing any blocks or baggage you have that is connected to other people, alive or dead, it is one of the most powerful.

We all need to have a personal investment in what we do. Sharing this information is mine.

1

Can You Afford Unforgiveness?

In ancient times, Hawai'i was almost completely devoid of mental and emotional diseases. If you read the earliest reports of the first missionaries and the first visitors to these islands, they found a group of people who were physically, emotionally, mentally, and spiritually very healthy. Of course, people did get sick and people got hurt, but health and wellness on all levels were the norm.

One of the most important spiritual teachers I have had in my life, Uncle George Na'ope, explained that the system in place to facilitate holistic healing at that time was so thorough and so complete that people experienced spiritual, mental, emotional, and physical wellness. He also pointed out that the Hawaiians' definition of "health" transcended the physical body.

One of the cornerstones of this system was the concept of being *pono*, for which there really is no good English translation. Basically, *pono* means to feel "right" with a person, with yourself, and even with the world. It did not mean right, as in "I'm right and you're wrong," but rather it's the sense that you are connected to and in harmony with nature, your community, your friends and family, and yourself. You feel at peace, comfortable in your own skin. You feel acceptance and appreciation for everything and everyone. You feel balanced and a profound sense that all is well. When you feel pono, you are connected to your heart, and your decisions and actions are driven by integrity and an awareness of what is good for the whole. Pono is feeling profound respect for all and, with it, a deep sense of self-respect.

But pono is not just a characteristic that you have or don't have or a badge you earn once and you're done. To be pono is an active process of staying aware of who you are being in the world. Are you acting in harmony with others? Do your choices reflect your deepest values? Are you being the best self you know how to be at this point in time?

John Ka'imikaua, one of my other spiritual teachers who began teaching at our Huna Workshop in the late '80s, had a very specific view on the importance of being pono. He said that for the ancient Hawaiians, being pono was not optional. It wasn't some distant state that you found only when sitting on your meditation pillow. It wasn't a feeling that you might have every once in a while if the stars aligned. Being pono was a basic necessity of everyday life. Ancient Hawaiians believed that being pono was critical to their physical, emotional, and mental health and that it was always in reach. When they did not feel pono, they recognized it as a sign that something was off, and they did something about it to bring themselves back into harmony.

And that something was ho'oponopono.

"Ho'o" means to make, so ho'oponopono means to "make right." When you double the word *pono*, you increase its meaning, so it's not just tolerating others but being in total harmony with them. It's not just feeling okay about yourself but feeling deep respect for who and what you are. It's not just giving lip service to your values but living them daily. It is being right with yourself and others on all levels.

When to Use Ho'oponopono

Ho'oponopono was, and is, primarily used in three instances:

The first instance is with **a person who has wronged you**, which is the bulk of the focus of this book. To become a doctor of integrative psychology, I did my dissertation research on ho'oponopono, using individuals who had been wronged by someone. That "someone" is called a transgressor, someone who has gone over your boundaries, who has done wrong to you. In my study, we measured unforgiveness.

Unforgiveness is holding onto the grudge. It's feeling "I want to get away from you. I want to get you back. Whenever I think of you and what you did, I get furious." After our subjects experienced the process of ho'oponopono, we were able to measure a statistically significant reduction in that grudge or that feeling of unforgiveness. To put it in plain English, people were pissed off, and after ho'oponopono they were no longer pissed off at that person who overran their boundaries.

Tony Robbins now talks about ho'oponopono from his stage, and about how it helped to heal a negative situation in his life. Joe Vitale worked with Dr. Hew Len, and Dr. Hew Len studied with a lady named Morrnah Simeona (with whom my father also studied), and Morrnah Simeona dedicated her life to teaching ho'oponopono. For all of them, the primary focus has been on using ho'oponopono for a transgression. So, even though there are other times to use ho'oponopono, much of the material on ho'oponopono has that same focus of working with someone who has wronged you.

In ancient times in Hawai'i, you also did ho'oponopono with **someone you loved** because you wanted to be connected with them and to deepen and improve your relationship.

As I write this, my son is seventeen, a young man now, yet I remember him clearly as a very young boy. When I wrote my first book, *The Foundation of Huna*, he was a child, and I wrote about him in that book. My daughter had just been born. I love those memories of my children being young, and I don't want to see them as babies anymore. I want to see them growing up, becoming young adults; therefore, I do ho'oponopono on a regular basis with them to reconnect with them as they grow and become older.

We'll discuss in this book reasons why you would do this with someone you love, someone that you are connected with, and the benefits of it, as well as stories of people who have utilized this in their relationships.

The third situation where you would use hoʻoponopono is with **someone who has passed away**. In the ancient culture of Hawaiʻi, it was taught that when someone passed away, what you were connected with is now an empty vessel with no energy coming back to you (we'll talk about energy in Chapter Five). You want to release the person who has died and let this person live on in your memories.

To become pono with them is to gain completion. So in the case of a death, the process is about gaining completion, becoming pono with the loss of this person, then connecting with them in your memories.

The Gifts of Hoʻoponopono

So why is hoʻoponopono most commonly referred to as a forgiveness process when you use it with loved ones even when something isn't necessarily wrong? Even when things are amazing with my kids or my partner, I still do this process on a regular basis. Therefore, even if something isn't wrong and you are doing hoʻoponopono, why is it still called forgiveness? I think this will be clear to you by the end of the book. The importance of this is that hoʻoponopono gives you two gigantic gifts.

The first gift is that hoʻoponopono helps you maintain your energy and your own personal vitality. It allows you to disconnect with other individuals who might drain your energy.

I know many other teachers who do the type of work I do. Some of them who are my age get totally wiped out from teaching. One teacher I know teaches a five-day training, then has to "hide out" at home in solitude for two weeks to recover energetically.

As I'm writing this book, I just completed teaching a series of trainings pretty much nonstop for the past five months, and I still have plenty of energy, time, and vitality. I credit a lot of that to ho'oponopono.

The second gift of ho'oponopono is emotional healing. Emotional healing doesn't mean you will never have negative emotions. It means that you have an easier time accessing positive, beautiful emotions and an easier time releasing negative ones. Almost every spiritual teacher on the planet says to increase your experiences of love, joy, and happiness, and to decrease your experiences of negative emotions that take away from the positive ones.

In Chapter Four, we'll talk about baggage and how it affects you physically, mentally, and emotionally. I think we all know, at the deepest level of who we are, that holding onto your baggage and negativity hurts only one individual—you.

So to me, the benefit of ho'oponopono is two-pronged. First, it helps you to maintain your energy and become more spiritually aware of the gifts of forgiveness. Secondly, emotionally you have less baggage and you become a more forgiving person in general. As we all know, energy and emotions dramatically affect every area of our life. This process is a true gift and an opportunity for you not just to heal but also to begin to take back control over your energy and your energy connections.

What Is Unforgiveness Costing You?

If you are holding onto unforgiveness, what is it costing you?

For my PhD dissertation on hoʻoponopono, I had to do what's called a literature review, which is a fancy way of saying, "giving credit to all the people that have already done a ton of research on forgiveness." It also allowed me to learn what is currently known about forgiveness and the effects of not forgiving, otherwise known as unforgiveness.

I found so much information and so many studies that I had to be picky. A ton of information and research validates that holding onto the grudge, holding onto unforgiveness harms the body, period. Holding onto the baggage hurts only you. It does not hurt anyone else.

For example, studies show that holding onto the unforgiveness increases stress levels. The moment stress levels increase, you sleep less, you have digestion-related issues, you prematurely age, and a series of heart-related and immune-system issues develop. This is all well documented and very clear.

The research also points toward unforgiveness causing cultural harm. In one of the studies that I cited in my dissertation, the only process that was healing the pain and trauma of the atrocities that occurred in Rwanda was a forgiveness process. It wasn't hoʻoponopono. It was a process that was indigenous to Rwanda, yet it was so extremely similar to hoʻoponopono that it was magical. The people most deeply affected by the genocide who were having the most difficulty physiologically and emotionally gained the biggest and fastest benefits. It was about forgiveness. It was about forgiving the people who had done horrible things to others.

In one of the case studies that I reviewed, a mom had lost her son to a murderer. At the end of the trial, she stood and looked at the person who had just been convicted of taking her son's life. She said, "I now have to forgive you so that I can be free of this." Then she said, "Please forgive me too."

Some people won't understand this, but she stood up in court and said, "I forgive you and please forgive me because I held onto such negativity towards you. And I realize now that you're a human being, and that you need to experience your path now and the repercussions of this. And I need to be free of it." So she said in open court, "I forgive you."

In interview after interview in case studies, people who have been the most deeply affected by horrific experiences know intuitively that holding onto that unforgiveness could literally kill them. They are determined to let it go. People on the periphery, however, often have trouble with it. The periphery people who stood behind this mother in court held up signs saying, "Kill him. Bring back the death penalty." These are the people who are determined to hang on to their anger for decades.

As a teacher of ho'oponopono, and having taught it now for twenty years, I find it interesting that the people most deeply affected by horrific events are the first to want to let it go, while other people just want to hold onto the negativity, even sometimes on behalf of the person who was actually wronged. It may be that the people who are hit the hardest by horrific things recognize forgiveness as a life-and-death decision, whereas those on the periphery or who experienced a lesser wrong don't have that same life-or-death feeling about it.

Holding onto unforgiveness increases stress, reduces your immune capabilities, interrupts your sleep, and is related to heart disease. And the studies go on and on. Even though holding onto it hurts only one person—you—some people still choose not to forgive based on various misconceptions. We'll talk about these misunderstandings in the next chapter.

2

What Forgiveness Is and Isn't

E kala mai ia'u.

There was no direct or specific way to say "sorry" in Hawaiian. Instead, you would ask for forgiveness. The phrase above is Hawaiian and means "Please forgive me," and that forgiveness is a process, not an end state. So what is forgiveness?

There are two major types of forgiveness. The first one is "episodic forgiveness," which is a fancy psychological way of saying, "A negative event occurred, and to gain resolution on it, a part of the process of gaining resolution can include forgiveness."

In my humble opinion, resolution really must include forgiveness—forgiveness of a person, forgiveness of a situation, forgiveness of the self. When someone hurts you or a negative situation occurs, you begin to hold onto that unforgiveness, that grudge, that negative emotion. It could be an anger. It could be a sadness, even fear. Forgiveness is the release of those emotions.

Ho'oponopono is most useful in working with these types of emotions when they are tied to individuals or groups of people. Other Hawaiian techniques help release general anger, sadness, or fear, but ho'oponopono is the most effective process when another person is involved.

The other type of major forgiveness attribute (from a psychological perspective) is what's called "trait forgiveness," which is having the psychological trait of being a forgiving person. Undoubtedly you've noticed in your own experience that some people are simply more forgiving than others. When something bad happens to them, these people tend to look at the positive side of things. They seem to take things less personally and aren't easily offended. They might be better at seeing another person's point of view or understanding where the transgressor is coming from. Someone with trait forgiveness is generally better able to overcome difficult or stressful situations.

One of the studies that I reviewed for my dissertation found that a person who practices episodic forgiveness on a regular basis begins to develop trait forgiveness. In plain English, someone who gains the power to forgive in specific situations begins to become a more forgiving person in general. That's a powerful learning. Practicing forgiveness teaches you and gives you the tools to become calm and more congruent, to become what the Hawaiians describe as *malie*, meaning to be calm, relaxed.

We can all benefit from being more *malie*. Modern life has lots of potential stress triggers: getting stuck in traffic, missing your bus, being interrupted while speaking, facing angry customers, being disrespected at work. We have all seen someone interpret these types of events in an extremely negative way, having a minor meltdown over something that seems inconsequential. Doesn't it make you want to just reach out to them and hug them and hold them and tell them that it's not that bad, that everything will be fine?

Yet some people can completely lose it with these daily annoyances. In one area, I used to be one of them: I used to have the most horrific attitude toward TSA (Transportation Security Administration) agents. It started when I was flying with my son who was five at the time, and it was not too long after 9/11. I was randomly selected to be searched.

The TSA agent, who was very new, said, "You've been randomly selected. We also have to pat down your son."

I said, "Great. Let me just explain to him what's going to happen."

But he stopped me, saying, "TSA protocol—you're not allowed to talk to the person. If you do, we'll isolate you."

I started to get ticked. "He's only five. He wasn't even picked." Then the TSA agent began to threaten that they would detain me and not let me on my plane.

As a parent, I was naturally angry and fearful. My son was crying, they were patting him down, and the TSA agent was threatening to call Child Protective Services if I opened my mouth again. Finally, the supervisor came over and rectified the situation, giving me all sorts of explanations for their actions but never apologizing. I was looking for the apology that we all look for, but I never got it, which left a bad taste in my mouth. I developed a negative opinion of the TSA and most especially of their agents.

I did not do ho'oponopono on the incident. I got rid of what I thought was the baggage using other techniques and simply forgot to do ho'oponopono. I thought I was done, yet every time I showed up at a TSA checkpoint, I'd have another negative experience. I didn't like what occurred. I didn't like who I'd become in those situations. I even talked about it during my trainings, making jokes about those "lame" TSA agents.

We absolutely create our reality through our beliefs. Students would come up to me and make negative comments about TSA, and I would agree with them. One guy told me that TSA agents are paid worse than Starbucks employees, and that Starbucks employees have better training. I looked it up, and it was true!

And I felt vindicated. "There you go. Proof." My perception of the situation, my reality, grew and grew. Then one day, years later, as I'm picking my daughter up from school, the classroom mom walked around the corner. She is an amazing woman. I've always thought of her as smart and empowered, just a wonderful person, and there she was, coming around the corner wearing a TSA uniform!

I looked at her. As gifted as I've learned to be with communication, I completely stuck my foot clear down my throat. Before I could stop myself, I practically screamed, "No!"

She looked down at her uniform, and she looked at me with a sarcastic smile and said, "Yes."

"No! Why are you a TSA agent?" I asked. "You're too nice."

She smiled and said, "Matt, we're human, too."

I shook my head. "I don't know. I really don't know."

Then she asked, "Why do you have such a negative opinion of TSA agents?"

I said, "I travel a lot."

She smiled again and said, "I know. I've seen you."

I was confused. "But I've never seen you there."

She nodded. "Oh, I waved at you a couple times. You just didn't notice." It dawned on me that I was so into my TSA story at the airport I hadn't even seen her there.

She continued, "You know, it's tough for some of us. Imagine going to work, and for eight hours, people show up and they already hate you, and they've never met you. How would you like that?" I couldn't imagine someone hating her. If they only knew her! But I realized that I had shown up in those TSA lines hating people I didn't know too.

She said, "We don't look forward to a lot of the things that we have to do. But it's our job." Then she hugged her daughter, a great little girl I adore. "I do it for her."

I realized that I had been holding onto a grudge. By then, my son was in the fifth or sixth grade and had no residual trauma from that event years before. I had no reason to hold onto that unforgiveness.

So I did a whole other level of release work on it and finally did ho'oponopono. The next time I was at the airport, a thought suddenly occurred to me: "These people don't set goals to mess with us. They don't have a deep desire to give ten pat-downs in a day. Nor do they pray that a few people haven't showered. They're doing a job—a thankless job." I began to notice things around me I hadn't noticed before when I was wrapped in my attitude that TSA agents were all out to get me.

I began to treat TSA agents like human beings. I memorized their names, said hi to them, and thanked them, not in a disingenuous way, but with sincerity. "Hey, thank you for doing what you're doing, man. It seems like a thankless job."

When I saw one TSA agent getting yelled at by the person in front of me, I walked up, looked the agent in the eye, and said, "They'll never say this to you, but I will. That was uncalled for. If I could, on their behalf, I would say I'm sorry about that. I hope you forgive them and don't hold onto it. It's just not worth it."

I began to experience TSA checkpoints in a totally different way. One day when I had been randomly selected again, the person standing next to me who was also getting patted down was enraged, swearing under his breath at the person patting them down. He complained, "This has ruined my entire vacation," as if this one moment at the airport could ruin his whole experience.

I looked at the guy patting me down and thought, *I don't think he enjoys his job. I really don't. I know that's a mind-read, but he doesn't look thrilled to be patting me down or kneeling on the ground or any of this.*

By then, the guy standing next to me had raised his voice at the agent patting him down. The first thought that occurred to me was, *You don't yell at a guy whose hands are that high up on your thigh. It's just a logistical thing.* Suddenly, the guy turns to me and says, "What do you think?"

I just looked right back at him and said, "I think you've got to pay good money for this kind of attention in some places. At least, that's what I've heard."

The person patting me down looked up at me in shock. He paused, the look on his face telling me he was trying to figure out if he'd heard what he thought he did. Finally, he fell back on his ass, laughing hysterically. When he finally stopped laughing, he said, "Thank you for that. I'd had a really, really bad day. But you just made my week."

Later as I walked through the little airport in Kona, I ran into that grumpy traveler again. He was still telling everyone how getting patted down had ruined his vacation. His wife was begging him to stop. "Please, honey, let this go. We had the most beautiful experience. We went up to the volcano."

He turned to his wife and said, "Don't you remember? It rained the entire time."

She shook her head and said, "No, it was beautiful."

But he insisted, "It was awful. We went up the Mauna Kea, and there was dust everywhere." It was as if he began to review all his vacation experiences through a filter of negativity.

As a doctor of psychology, I can tell you that if you're in a negative state and begin to review memories, you will actually alter the content of those memories and make them negative. This guy showed me a classic example, right at the airport.

Trait forgiveness is when someone can handle a stressful situation and not let it completely derail their day. A person who is practicing forgiveness on a regular basis might get cut off on the freeway and wonder, "Is the person in a hurry because maybe they need to get somewhere? Maybe they're late for a job interview. Maybe their kid is sick, and they're rushing to pick them up. Maybe his wife is pregnant and about to deliver."

You never know. I remember speeding when my former wife called me and told me she was about to give birth to our daughter. I hit the gas pedal pretty hard, cut off a few people, and got some horns honking at me. But I rushed home because my girl was about to be born. The other drivers didn't see that. They saw a crazy driver who had done them wrong. I wonder if any of those people blamed me for their inability to bring their A-game to work that day.

We sometimes allow the littlest things to completely derail us. When you become more forgiving, you can free yourself of that. When you are less forgiving and hold onto grudges, you begin to see things and filter experiences through grudge-colored glasses. Holding a grudge even affects how you label your emotions.

For example, the part of the brain that lights up when you have anxiety is the same part of the brain that lights up when you have excitement. It's the same part that lights up when you have anticipation. A person who filters everything through negativity will call it anxiety. A person with a more positive attitude will call it excitement or anticipation.

It's the difference between seeing that glass as half-empty or half-full. The moment you label your experiences and your emotions, you will see a trickle-down effect. Your physical body will begin to change and different neurotransmitters will fire.

I could dive into all the scientific explanations of exactly how and why that happens, but let's just keep it simple. A person who holds onto unforgiveness and negativity becomes more negative. A person who holds onto a positive outlook and forgiveness becomes more forgiving.

I would rather live the rest of my life in the illusion that everyone around me is going through something, that their act wasn't an intentional violation of my personal experience, and that it was an accident, a mistake.

They missed the target just a little bit, or they went overboard. I'd prefer to forgive them and move on rather than die thinking the world is out to get me and TSA agents somehow have a personal vendetta against me. I'd rather die appreciating that the mom of one of my daughter's really good friends is a great person, even though she randomly pats people down and gets no thank-you.

Misconceptions About Forgiveness

This is important because right now, many of you are thinking, "I am ready to forgive everyone except that one jerk. That one person doesn't deserve it, and I don't ever want to be happy with them."

The biggest stumbling blocks to forgiving are the major misconceptions people often have. The first one is that forgiveness somehow means you are supposed to be buddies with your transgressor again. Forgiveness doesn't require that at all.

I have forgiven the person who patted down my five-year-old. I am free of the baggage that unforgiveness created. I now know many TSA agents by name. When I show up at airports, even airports I haven't been to for a while, some of them will remember me and say, "Where you off to today, Doc?"

There's a guy in San Diego named Genesis who works for Hawaiian Airlines. I saw someone in front of me yell at him and treat him in the most horrific possible way, as if he wasn't even human. When I came up to the counter, I spent ten minutes just talking with him. When I passed through San Diego again, I hadn't seen him for months. But when I showed up, he said, "Dr. James, I'm so glad there's no one in front of you trying to make us both angry." I gave him a big handshake—one of those half-bro-man hugs.

To this day, if he's there when I go to the San Diego airport, he'll greet me with respect, not because I'm anyone important, but because one day he was having a rough time, and we were able to overcome it just through conversation. Guess what, though? I doubt he'd ever want to see that person who yelled at him again.

All that said, the guy who patted down my five-year-old? I'm not going to invite him over to dinner. I've forgiven him, but I still don't want to hang out with him.

I have had to let people go from my company. I hate doing that; it's a terrible experience. Every time I let someone go, I try to give them a hug on their way out and thank them for everything they've done. Yet even after doing ho‘oponopono and forgiving them, I still don't want them to be a part of the company.

Uncle George Na‘ope taught me that the first time someone does something wrong, you can say to them, "Shame on you." The second time someone does something wrong you can only say, "Shame on me." And in both instances, if your goal is to be done with a person, then you want to do it in a way that is pono.

You don't need to hang on to negative feelings about someone to maintain your boundaries. You can hold boundaries in a positive way. The Hawaiians have a saying, "Aloha ke akua," which on one level of translation means, "Love comes from above. Love comes from God. Love comes from spirit." On another level of translation (from Kumu Etua Lopes, one of my teachers), it also means that if you ever have to put up a shield, put it up as a shield of love.

When you hold onto unforgiveness, you try to kick people in the ass on their way out the door, which is counterproductive to your life and theirs. When you gain forgiveness with someone, you can still show them the door and thank them on their way out, or at the very least, be respectful of the fact that it's done.

If someone has wronged you, forgiveness means you free yourself of the baggage and gain the deeper lesson. Then you never need to see them again if that's your choice. However, I'd suggest you make that choice *after* you have gained forgiveness.

The second stumbling block to forgiveness is the misconception that holding onto your grudge will somehow make them suffer. Sorry, it just doesn't work that way.

During a training in Los Angeles, as I was about to take a group through this process, a lady raised her hand and said, "I don't think I'm ready to do this. I think my husband needs to suffer some more."

With a big, gentle smile, I looked at her from the stage, and I said, "Ma'am, how does your holding onto this cause him to suffer in any way, shape, or form?"

She took a deep breath and got ready to answer. Then she stopped and said, "It doesn't. It really doesn't."

I said, "Yeah, I really know. Unforgiveness only hurts you. You only harm yourself by holding onto it," I explained. "And is your husband the type of person that would want you to suffer some more?"

She nodded and said, "Yeah."

"Well, this is going to sound kind of twisted, and you may not understand it now," I said, "but you will get it later: forgiveness is one of the sweetest forms of revenge."

That may sound weird to you, but when a person is hanging on to a load of negativity and baggage, it does make sense to them. They're still in the stage of wanting to get back at the person who harmed them, so I explain that one way to get back at them is to let go of the unforgiveness and be free of it. Of course, after letting go of that baggage, they discover that there's no reason to get back at the other person after all!

Be clear with the fact that you're not causing your transgressor any discomfort or harm by holding onto your grudge, and you're not opening yourself or making yourself more vulnerable or giving in or having to become their friend. You're freeing you. You are freeing yourself from the baggage.

You are releasing it and becoming pono. You're becoming free. And when you do and the baggage is gone, you might decide that you don't need that person in your life anymore, and you'll do it in a way that's positive and congruent. There's nothing the other person can fight because they'll see that you're done.

The Problem with I'm Sorry

The Hawaiian alphabet consists of seven consonants (plus an okina or glottal stop) and five vowels, so they needed to be very clear with their language. Root languages, such as Hawaiian, are based on energy, and the energy of communication always flows back and forth between people: You make a connection to a person. The person makes a connection back to you. That's a circuit.

The Hawaiians didn't believe in saying "I'm sorry." According to Uncle George, who was fluent in the ancient Hawaiian language, there was no way to say, "I'm sorry" in the ancient Hawaiian language, and the problem with saying "I'm sorry" is that quite often, the response can be a negative response—or none at all.

(I would like to clarify the concept of "ancient" versus "modern". Having grown up in Hawai'i, I can tell you that things are very western and modern there now. Especially on Oahu. In the 70's I lived near a pig farmer and grew up in a rural area. The elders I studied with talked about ancient times and how things were and what could and couldn't be said and done. Today, the primary language is English and even most locals say, "I am sorry". There are still elders and teachers that emphasize the importance of forgiveness; however, it is not as prevalent as it was in ancient times where you could not even say the word sorry.)

You've undoubtedly had someone say, "I'm sorry" to you and thought, "Oh, not sorry enough," or "You will be sorry," or "Yeah, you are sorry, you sorry son-of-a-blank!"

The problem with "I'm sorry" is it's a statement of being that ends energetically about twelve inches from your mouth. When I share this on TV and radio shows, I tell people all the time to give up saying "I'm sorry," or if you say, "I'm sorry," back it up with "Please forgive me." When you say to someone "Please forgive me" and give them forgiveness back, it creates an energetic connection and allows forgiveness to take place.

That's why the Hawaiians say, "E kala mai ia'u," which means "Please forgive me." It gives the gift of forgiveness in a loving way, and then begs a response.

When my daughter was in preschool, I taught her the phrase "Please forgive me." I remember a time when she was in the kitchen and accidently knocked over some cereal one morning. She looked up at me and said, "Daddy, I'm sorry, please forgive me." I was in the middle of doing something and did not answer right away, and she just stood there, waiting for a response. I did not see it as such a big deal, because we all knock things over; however, it was a big deal to her and she was waiting for a response. As a parent, I needed to say to her, "I forgive you, Skylar. Now we need to have a discussion about being careful." We did, and it was a nice discussion.

The ball is in the other person's court when you say, "Please forgive me." When you say, "I'm sorry," nothing goes out to them. They aren't compelled to respond or engage in the forgiveness circuit you want to establish. So before you even jump to how to do ho'oponopono, begin to develop the mind-set of "Please forgive me; I forgive you," and notice what a difference it makes.

I'll sometimes take students through an exercise where they just sit for a while and think about what a game changer it would be to practice forgiveness spiritually, emotionally and within their language. They are fast to realize that getting rid of "I'm sorry" is not going to be a huge loss.

As we delve deeper into the concept of forgiveness and becoming pono, take some time to contemplate what it would mean to be free of the baggage towards another or even towards yourself. Be ok letting go of transgression and embracing forgiveness. As it should be clear now, holding onto it only hurts you.

3

Being Pono

We talked a little about what it means to be pono earlier. When you are pono, you have unwavering congruency. You are congruent inside and free of the negativity, free of the baggage.

Forgive and Forget – Being Pono with Others

When a person is pono with another person, nothing needs to be said again. When two people fight then truly forgive each other and move past the experience, if the subject ever does come up again, it doesn't come up as a fight. It comes up as an experience, and it comes up as a lesson.

"Hey, remember when we were driving in Minnesota and we learned that valuable lesson to let the driver know ahead of time when we're coming up to a gas station?" as opposed to, "You remember that time you yelled at me? Where you got all bent out of shape just because I forgot to mention that the gas station we just passed was the last for miles and miles?" Once you have truly forgiven, you are out of blamer mode and paying attention only to the lesson.

One of my students who taught Huna for a while with me was Sally Bishop. She used to say, "To forgive and to not forget is to never forgive in the first place." What she meant by that is that we need to forgive and forget.

Some people have a hard time with the forgetting part. "But what if the person did something really wrong? Don't you need to remember that?"

You need to remember the deeper lesson, not the incident itself. Hawaiians have a saying, "Ano'ai." Ano is a seed. Ai means to eat. "Eat the seed." In every situation there's a seed of knowledge, a seed of empowerment, and you're meant to bring that seed in.

When you've become pono with a negative experience, you forget the negative aspects of it, and you remember the lesson.

My daughter and I had a rough time once while traveling. After a while, I forgot the circumstances around the negative experience, but I remember the lesson: During travel sometimes, my daughter gets to be a little bit more sensitive, and I need to be sensitive of her needs. How can I be there to assist her as the adult, as the guide, as the father?

The next time we travelled together, we went to Italy, which is a very long trip from Hawai'i and a twelve-hour time-zone difference. Regardless, my daughter and I had a great time and a completely different experience. When you are pono with someone, nothing needs to be said. You have what's called unwavering congruency.

Pono with Yourself

When you're pono with yourself, you know who you are, and because you know who you are, you know what you're meant to do. That saying, "If you love what you do, you'll never have to work another day in your life," is only true when what you do flows from the essence of who you are.

In the three books I wrote on finding a deeper purpose in life (see Resource Section at the end of this book), I explain how to connect with that essence. I reference ho'oponopono in them because when a person knows who they are, it's easier for them to decide what it is that they're meant to do. When you're *not* pono with yourself, you often try to do things for the wrong reason.

For many years, I wasn't pono with my body. I had carried a lot of baggage, and I went from being a varsity athlete all the way up to 235 pounds. I was hauling around an extra 100 pounds of fat, and I wasn't pono with myself. I began to get more in control of my health, but I fell into the yo-yo diet syndrome, where I'd lose a lot of weight, feel really good, then all of a sudden, I'd pack it all back on again.

I took a look at myself, and I took a look at my experience. I realized that a lot of what I was doing to improve my body and health was actually for others. I was trying to get my students to think I looked good or trying please other people. I still wasn't pono with myself, even when

I was getting healthier and healthier. When I stopped caring about what other people thought and I became pono with my body, that's when I actually gained positive traction in health and fitness and shifted everything.

To become pono with my body, I used a few different processes to release emotional baggage and align my values. I used ho'oponopono, not to forgive my big tummy or fat thighs, but to forgive others: people who had teased me relentlessly, people who had said negative things about my body, people who tried to get me to look a certain way rather than seeing me for who I am. Ho'oponopono is a process of forgiveness with others, and we experience our life through other people. So while you can't become pono with a specific body part through ho'oponopono, you can become pono with the people that made you think that other people's opinions matter when they really don't.

More than ten years later, I've been able to maintain my health. What other people think of my body doesn't matter to me. I'm pono with me, and I'm pono with my path and what I do to be healthy. That's what pono means.

Getting Your Life Back by Becoming Pono

In 2015, I ran one of my NLP (neuro linguistics programing) practitioner trainings in San Diego. In every one of these trainings, I take the group through the process of ho'oponopono. The following is one of a few hundred powerful experiences I have been blessed to share with my students. In this example, we felt it best not to reveal the student's real name because of the nature of the experience. Therefore, in the book, I will refer to her as *Diane*.

A student named Diane raised her hand and said, "What if I don't know who wronged me?"

I responded, "I don't usually need detail, but I don't understand your question. How can you not know?" This young lady wore her hair pulled back and no makeup, and was wearing overalls and very dark colors—as well as a very stern look on her face.

She said, "I was in the Army, and my first night in the barracks, I was given the date-rape drug. I was raped, and I don't remember my attacker." She said, "And I need to be free of this. I'm ready to let it go."

I had already explained to the class that part of ho'oponopono is that you say, "I forgive you" to the person who wronged you. Then you say, "Please forgive me, too." I explained to Diane that, at the unconscious level in the subconscious, where you keep track of your energy connections, you know the connection. You may not know his name, but the connection is still there. "So you're going to have to trust the process and trust that your unconscious mind has that connection because it is there. Are you ready to be free of this?"

Diane said, "Yes, and I'm going to trust the process." It made perfect sense to her.

The lady sitting next to her, however, raised her hand, and in a most indignant tone said, "Why the hell does she need to say to her rapist, 'Please forgive me, too'?" This woman was seriously pissed off!

41

Before I could answer, Diane turned to her and said, "I don't care. I need to be free of this. It's going to kill me if I hold onto this, and I know it."

I thought, *Whoa. Well, that pretty much answers the question.* But I had to answer it for the rest of the people in the room and the lady sitting next to her, who was stunned.

So I told them about a criminal profiling class I'd taken that had a lot of FBI agents in it. A renowned teacher of both criminal profiling and the criminal mind-set taught the class. He told us, "As twisted and crazy as this sounds, even the most horrific criminal thinks that the person that they're doing the crime to deserves it and/or that they are justified in their actions." In their mind, because of this "deserved" aspect to it, they believe they're not doing anything wrong, that it's somehow okay and maybe even beneficial to society.

Think of the person who shot Ronald Reagan; he believed he was doing it for a valid reason. He believed that President Regan deserved it. So the insane part is, from Diane's attacker's perspective, maybe she did something wrong. I know that sounds terrible, and it pains me to even say it. In looking at cases like this from a psychological perspective, many attackers have this twisted view. I've worked with individuals who have gone through some horrific things. Maybe you're asking for forgiveness for the perpetrator's own perception. It doesn't mean you have to agree with it.

Another perspective, and one that is much more appropriate and easier to understand, is that maybe after the horrific event that happened to you, you did something or said something you wish you hadn't. So, from that perspective, you're asking forgiveness for your reaction, meaning that after this terrible, unthinkable event, you have since acted, thought, and felt in ways that require forgiveness.

There's a beautiful book called *The Little Soul and the Sun*. It's a short story about these two souls who come together. The first soul needs a lesson in life, and the other soul says, "I'll help you experience that lesson because I love you so much." They hug, and the second soul says, "I'm going to do this lesson, and I'm going to help you gain this lesson, but please just remember I'm doing it because I love you."

The other soul looks at the second soul and says, "What do you mean?" The second soul responds, "Well, in order for you to get this lesson in this lifetime, I'm going to have to be someone that's not so nice. I'm going to have to be someone that you're actually going to hate."

"Deep down inside, we made this agreement, and we're going to forget that we made this agreement. And you're going to have this experience so that you can grow and evolve as a soul. And I'm sorry that I'm doing it to you, and I'm just doing it because we decided that that would be a lesson that you wanted to get."

I learned this powerful story from Tris Thorp, an inspiring colleague of mine who has been teaching with Deepak Chopra for close to a decade. She does a lot of high-end coaching and happens to be the woman I am in an amazing relationship with. She tells this story to a lot of her students and clients to illustrate that the person who wronged you may have given you the biggest lesson in your life and that maybe on some level, you needed that lesson.

I'm not claiming that the awful things people do are right or wrong or happy or sad or good or bad. What I'm saying is that I've met people who have been through some horrific things in their lives, and when they're able to become free of the baggage and to become pono with what happened, they often feel like they've gained some amazing wisdom and even purpose to their lives.

Again, I want to repeat that being pono with what happened and with the perpetrators doesn't mean you are buddies with them again. You don't need to hang out with someone who attacked you. Pono means that you're free of the negative emotions. You're free of the baggage. When you're pono and you're free of it, some of those most horrific events in life become our biggest lessons, our most important experiences.

I've worked with people who have been through things I can't comprehend, and I see them come through the other side and become a beacon of light, showing the way for other people. They help other people and guide them through tough times. I've never met anyone who, once they are free of their baggage, would trade in their experiences and the wisdom they've been given.

Once you are free of the baggage, it's okay to move forward, and it doesn't mean that you want to experience it again. It means that you gained that deeper lesson.

So after Diane told us about her horrific experience, the cover-up that followed, and how she was treated, she looked at the person sitting next to her and said, "I'll say it. I will say, 'Please forgive me,' because I will die if I can't be free of this baggage."

Diane did the process one time through with the class, came up to me that evening, gave me a big hug, and went home. The next day, she showed up with makeup on and her hair down, wearing a dress, and she had a glow of happiness and joy. People in the training went up to her, hugged her, and thanked her for sharing. She inspired an entire group of people she'd never known before, and she went on to take a few more trainings with me.

A year after that experience, Diane assisted one of my trainings in San Diego. I asked her to share her story with the group because I tell Diane's story at every single one of my events during ho'oponopono.

That day, she shared something I didn't know. She said, "I was ready to kill myself. This process saved me. Some people don't understand why I had to say, 'Please forgive me,' to the person who raped me, who brutalized me, who did the most horrific thing you can think of."

"I had to say it because I became such a negative person afterwards in the way that I behaved, and I did things toward him and other people. I needed to be free of that, too, and I needed to be forgiven. It is a two-way street."

She shared with the group how her life has completely changed. She's happy now and has joy in her life, and while she would never wish the experience upon anyone, she would never trade in what happened. It's made her appreciate life at a whole other level. Diane now helps and guides other people to overcome their baggage and is one of these shining stars who doesn't complain about the petty things that most of us often complain about.

Think of that person whose day is ruined when they go to the coffee shop, order almond milk, and are given soy milk instead. Diane can laugh about those kind of things—"I guess I was supposed to have soy today!"—and move on.

Diane gained that level of resolution during her one session. But to maintain pono with yourself, and pono with your past, and pono with your experiences, you have to practice it on a regular basis. A different person will wrong or hurt you. Another event will upset you. You'll get knocked off center by something or someone. When I'm asked what is required to stay pono, it's consistent practice.

There's a great book called *The Slight Edge* by a guy named Jeff Olson. He says that successful people do little things every day that led to their being successful. To get to where I have gotten in my life, my daily practice includes ho'oponopono, and it includes forgiveness.

This practice has impacted every single area of my life in the most positive, beautiful way possible. We all know that if you want to be physically fit, you need to eat more than just one salad. You can't eat a salad and say, "I'm done. Health is now mine." Physical health is about consistency.

Hoʻoponopono should be a part of your consistent diet for spiritual and emotional health and well-being. When you do that, it transforms the other areas as well.

(For more information on the Hawaiian concept of pono, please see the Resources Section at the end of this book.)

4

Our Emotional Baggage

The person who taught my father about Huna and ho'oponopono was Papa Bray. David Bray Jr. was his English name. Papa Bray used the terminology that his father, David "Daddy" Bray, used to describe what in contemporary language we often call emotional baggage: black bags.

Papa Bray explained that black bags were those things we carry inside us that we need to free ourselves from. He explained that it doesn't mean that the color black is good or bad, but in life, our goal is to stand in *ao,* which means the light. One of the things we need to do is learn how to stand in our light and expand that light. Our black bags are the absence of the light.

Baggage is just trapped energy—and that's the easiest way to think of it: trapped energy.

Choosing the Light

A student once sent me an e-mail asking, "How do I fight the darkness? I see so much darkness out there, so much darkness in the world. How do I fight the darkness?" I found the question to be very interesting, but I don't like to answer questions if I don't understand the reality of the person asking me the question.

At the time, I was sitting on the couch with my son sitting next to me. He looked over at me, and I must have had a funny look on my face. "Dad, are you okay?"

I said, "Yeah, Ethan, I'm okay. I just got this really weird question. I don't know how to answer it."

I just sat thinking about fighting the darkness. What type of mind-set do you have to have to go out there and fight darkness? Everything that I've ever learned growing up is that if you go to fight something, you become the thing you're fighting. If you put energy into that, you become that thing. In my book *Integrate the Shadow*, I talk about the darker things that we can become that we claim we are not.

Mother Teresa refused to participate in an antiwar rally because it can take on a warlike mentality and can become dark (not always, but the potential is there), but she would participate in a pro-peace rallies. It's not just splitting hairs. Fighting *against* something and being *for* something are completely different mind-sets and very different energies.

So I sat there, lost in thought, trying to sort it out, when Ethan said, "Isn't it trash night, Dad?" I snapped back to reality, bundled up the garbage, and walked outside.

It was one of those moments when nature shows you how beautiful it is and how magnificent it truly can be. It was totally dark outside and a fog had rolled in. I live at a 2,500-foot elevation on the island of Hawai'i. It was either a new moon or the moon hadn't yet come up, resulting in the total darkness.

I couldn't see anything, so I waited for my eyes to adjust. It was so dark, though, that even when my eyes adjusted, I still couldn't see. So I stood there in awe, enjoying the beauty of that moment. Finally, my arm started getting tired, so I took a step forward. After a few paces, I hit the motion sensor, and a bright light shined down from the flood lamps.

As I walked into this circle of light, a new phenomenon occurred. I looked around, and it was the most interesting thing I had ever seen. Just beyond the ring of light coming from the flood lamp, just where the light ended, I could see fog for about two feet. Then it went into total darkness, and I couldn't see anything beyond that.

It was as if the light had created a natural barrier. It hit me that in the middle of the brightest day, darkness can't do that. Darkness can't shine down a cone of darkness and block out the light. And I realized that a person's path doesn't need to include *fighting* the darkness.

A person needs to know how to step fully into their light and expand that light because the darkness has no power within the light. Darkness cannot enter into the light unless you allow it.

That's why emotional baggage is called a black bag in my lineage of Huna, because when we carry emotional baggage from the past, we're carrying darkness inside us. "Baggage" is a simple way of stating we're carrying a negative emotion—anger, sadness, fear, guilt. We're carrying the grudge, the unforgiveness, and we're holding it in our body. By holding onto it, we are allowing the darkness to come into our light. One of the main problems with that is that you begin to see—all around you—the darkness you carry inside you.

Your Baggage Shapes Your Reality

Dr. Bruce Lipton worked as a faculty member at the university I ran prior to his book *Biology of Beliefs* really taking off. I recently spent some time with him again, and he told my son, "Your dad and your grandfather helped to launch my career." I felt very grateful that he remembered our time together and that my son got to meet him. He is an amazing person.

Michael Beckwith had invited Dr. Lipton to speak at Agape, and I was able to meet Michael too. That night, Dr. Lipton was attempting to get a point across that a part of the function of our unconscious mind is to make our reality reflect our beliefs. It's like a self-fulfilling prophecy.

If you believe that the opposite sex is untrustworthy, unreasonable, self-centered, or _____ (fill in the blank), eventually you'll experience that quality in every one of the opposite sex you meet—even when that experience isn't necessarily real.

Once, after teaching a Huna weekend in Toronto, I came to Newport Beach to start off the next Huna weekend that I was doing. (I was doing back-to-back weekends, which is rare.) Because of the momentum and the amazing group I had in Toronto, I came in feeling fired up and feeling highly motivated.

I must have brought a lot of energy because two ladies walked up to me when we went on the lunch break the very first day to talk with me. The one standing to my right spoke first and said, "I'd like to introduce myself. My name is so-and-so, and I'm really, really happy to be here." I thanked her, and she continued, "I would like to humbly ask you to do me a huge favor." When I indicated I would, she said, "Will you tone it back a notch? You are one of the most aggressive spiritual teachers I have ever met in my life."

I took a deep breath and thought, *Wow. Oh man, I need to ask for forgiveness—not tell her she's wrong, not tell her she's right—just ask for forgiveness because that was her experience of it, and I have to honor her experience.*

Before I could say anything, the lady standing to my left, who had come up at the same time, turned to her and said, "What the hell have you been watching for the past two hours? This is the most passionate spiritual trainer I have met. I wish my spiritual teachers had this much passion and fun with what they do."

The first lady turned to her and said, "I don't think he was passionate. He was pretty aggressive. In fact, I think that he has a little bit of repressed anger. You know, most men do."

The second lady looked at her and said, "You clearly can't see energy because he has a golden aura, and he's got no baggage and no aggressiveness. He's a being of light." And they started arguing over who I am and how I felt and the color of my aura ...

I finally had to calm them down. "Ladies, that's really awesome that both of you shared this. This is going to be a fun experience."

"Look," I continued, "here's the deal: I wasn't feeling passionate, nor was I feeling aggressive. I was highly motivated. That's my term. That's my emotion, and yet you came up here with your labels, and you came up here with your perceptions."

The second lady said, "Yeah, all spiritual teachers, they have a deep passion." So of course, she saw my behavior as passionate because that was her model of the world. The first lady looked down at the ground and said, "I'm here because I have a lot of relationship issues, and I always think that men are overly aggressive. And I just put that onto you."

I said, "I forgive you, and I wasn't going to say that what you experienced was wrong. That was your experience. The valuable lesson the two of you need to gain here is that each of us can see the same thing and yet experience it differently. And if we carry baggage, we see our experiences through that baggage."

This is why, in the ancient Hawaiian culture, it was required that you let go of your baggage—because black bags are the absence of the light. You were required to become pono. You were not allowed to start a new path—new relationship, new job, new direction—unless you were pono.

In my book *The Foundation of Huna*, I talk about Uncle George, who was instrumental in my spiritual path, my spiritual teacher, my guide. Before Uncle George could become a teacher, he went and did release work with Daddy Bray. (Daddy Bray's son taught my father and gave permission for us to teach this lineage of energy work and Huna.) To become a teacher, Uncle George had to be free of his baggage because if he didn't release it, he knew he would see his students through the baggage.

An angry person tends to see the world around them through the filter of anger, a sad person through the filter of sadness.

Because I love to simplify things, I encourage you to think of baggage as your underlying emotional state or filter. Think of waking up on the wrong side of the bed in a grumpy mood. Now compare that to a day when you wake up filled with joy and happiness, feeling like nothing can go wrong. You could encounter the exact same experience on those two different days, but you'll label it and experience it completely differently because of the filter you started the day with.

Why Your Baggage Pops Up

Baggage becomes a filter. In ancient Hawai'i, you were required to let it go when it came up. On the path, our baggage will come up, sometimes very suddenly, as if from out of nowhere. Maybe it's a Pavlovian response: You hear a song and suddenly you're reminded of the love of your life who got away or dumped you. Maybe you smell baked goods and remember your mom, forgetting the negative times but remembering her sweetness, until suddenly, you start beating yourself up for not having said "I love you" one more time. Maybe you see something insignificant yet it enrages you, and you recognize that it's time to let your rage go.

In ancient Hawai'i, when all of these out-of-the-blue things would happen, you would celebrate it. You would go do a process. You'd go down to the beach and cry. You'd go to the volcano. You would release. You would let it go through ho'oponopono.

But in Western culture, we shove it back down. As one student screamed out during a training, "We medicate it! We medicate the baggage!" It's true; some people do medicate the baggage rather than deal with it. I don't have a negative viewpoint on medication. I believe that everything can serve a valuable purpose. However, we do live in a society that sometimes refuses to deal with the real source of their pain.

Many people are on medications and/or refusing to deal with their deeper issues, and it just gets worse and worse. We accumulate these tiny, little black bags that become trunk-loads of baggage that weigh us down and prevent us from moving forward.

My marriage of fourteen years ended, and we both celebrated the end. We both became pono with it. We then held space for people around us to heal. Some people couldn't understand why we didn't have negative emotions toward the divorce and each other. We're both now in happy relationships, have great communication with each other, and co-parent. We've moved on.

Letting go of your baggage can be the process of allowing a long path—a relationship, a career, an identity—to come to completion and end—in a positive way. You don't need to end things in a negative way.

Too many people take the opposite approach. They stay in a relationship too long only to get more and more bitter with their partner. Then one day, they leave the relationship, pissed off, and proclaim to the universe, "I will never let someone treat me like that again." Six months later, they get together with another person who looks different, maybe has different color hair, has a different name, but is the exact same person they left.

Deepak Chopra offered a beautiful saying in a private lecture: "You gain the lessons of second grade and graduate and go to third grade. And if you don't, you repeat second grade until you get it." I grew up in a society that only taught through stories, so I realized he was talking about relationships, and he was talking about careers, and he was talking about friends. He was talking about past lives.

He was saying that in life we're given opportunities to learn something. If we don't learn it, we keep repeating until we do. We keep getting into those crappy relationships. We keep getting into those dead-end jobs. We keep hanging out with those dead-beat friends. The funny thing is that these are all people who have agreed to give us lessons in our life. They bring up our baggage not because they are jerks. They bring it up because it's time for us to let it go.

Part of the job of your unconscious mind is to present baggage to you when it is ready for resolution. It sticks it right in your face so that you can't ignore it. Rather than seeing this as a negative thing, you want to see it as a positive thing because if you hold onto your baggage, it trickles down and affects your body.

The Journal of the *American Medical Association* published a study in 1994 that said holding onto anger increases heart-related disease. Studies have been around since the '80s and '90s showing how specific negative emotions harm the body. Sadness, when it becomes overwhelming, will actually begin to depress the body's immune system. Fear will heighten stress, change hormone levels, cause lack of sleep, and increase the likelihood of the onset of disease and sickness, even increasing the likelihood of things like the common cold or flu. The research is out there and has been for decades.

Is letting go of baggage the only thing that you need to do? No, you need to have a healthy body. You need to have a healthy emotional body, a healthy mental body, and a healthy spiritual body. I teach from a holistic model, and forgiveness plays a key role in this on all levels.

We can carry the baggage of past relationships, past jobs, past friends, past experiences, and tie it to a person, believing that the person was the one that had wronged us, only to one day wake up and realize we created those experiences for a deeper lesson. Baggage can come from a variety of different sources and prevent you from moving forward. When it accumulates, baggage becomes huge and weighs us down, preventing us from moving forward and having positive experiences.

Some people pick up and cling to their baggage as if it's the story of who they really are. I have met people who identify more with their baggage from the past than who they are in the present. They lead with it in almost every interaction.

When I meet certain people, the interaction goes like this: "Hi, so nice to meet you. My name is Dr. Matt. What's yours?" Within five seconds, they're telling me how they could have been so much more in life. They open up and dump out all their baggage about how awful things have been for them, all their illnesses, failures, missed opportunities. They may have terrific marriages and wonderful kids—but they identify most with the story of how tough life is.

To experience a fulfilling, empowered life, you need to get rid of your baggage. You need to be willing to let go of your negative stories and begin to tell positive stories and share positive experiences. I've never met someone who, at the end of their life, complained about enjoying or appreciating their lives or that they followed everything their heart desired. But I have met a lot of people who have regret.

So it's never too late to be free of the baggage and create an amazing present and even a wonderful past. When I let go of my baggage around specific family members, I began to remember things, positive times that I had completely forgotten. When you've released your negative filters and you're in a positive mood and standing in your light, you're flooded with happy memories, and you recall positive things.

Negative Emotion Versus Emotional Baggage

It's important to make the distinction between having a negative emotion and emotional baggage. Clearing your baggage does not mean that you'll never have a negative emotion again.

When my son got patted down by the TSA agent, in that moment, I was having a human response. I was angry. Five days later when I was still angry, I was turning the experience of that moment into baggage.

Our emotions of anger, fear, sadness, and even guilt are wired into us for a reason. They are signals that something is not right or off track or even dangerous in that moment. Emotional baggage, on the other hand, is about past experiences that you need to resolve or release, but you haven't yet. The inherent problem with hanging onto emotional baggage is that when you encounter a new experience that causes you to have a human response to something, your response draws up all of that old baggage, and its energy is added to your response. Your expression in the moment becomes the sum total of your present experience *plus* all your past experiences, and this is why people overreact to situations.

Take a person who has a lot of fear and has gone through experiences where they've been scared. If they refuse to let go of their past fear and cling to it instead, the moment when they become afraid, the energy of the present fear acts like a magnet and pulls up all the other baggage.

Having emotions in the moment is called being human. Doing hoʻoponopono, doing Huna or any of the other techniques that I teach, isn't going to stop you from having emotions in the moment. It's going to free you from the baggage that you've been holding onto that's ready to resolve, ready to release. It's going to free you so that you can have clear and healthy emotional experiences.

I do hoʻoponopono all the time. When Uncle George, my mentor and spiritual teacher, passed away in 2009, I felt huge sadness, and yet it was sadness just about Uncle George. It wasn't all the other sadness that I've ever felt; I had dealt with that. So this sadness was very specific. It was very profound.

And as powerful as it was from an emotional standpoint, it didn't overwhelm me. Some people get overwhelmed by their emotions not because they are weak as individuals, but because their emotional responses in the moment also include the emotional baggage from the past. Hoʻoponopono frees you from that baggage in the past.

(For more information about dealing with negative emotions, please see the Resources Section at the end of this book.)

5

Energy and the Part It Plays in Forgiveness

In my book *The Foundation of Huna*, I talk a lot about energy. I wrote that book early in my career, right after I had become *Kumu*, which in Hawaiian means "teacher." Earlier in my career, back in the '90s when I first started teaching NLP, we used to keep our talks on energy separate from everything else that we did.

People were not as familiar with the idea of energy back then. I remember this one young man at one of the trainings who said, "You know, your aloha shirts are okay, Dr. Matt. Your discussions on NLP and hypnosis are amazing. And I know you talk about that weird woo-woo energy stuff. You're not going to talk about any of that weird stuff here, are you?"

Then he raised a tiny red can up to his mouth and took a sip.

I stared at him for a second and said, "What weird stuff?"

"You know, about that woo-woo energy."

I said, "So you don't believe in energy?"

He shrugged. "Not at all, that stuff is just, you know, crystals and meditation." (Remember, this was the '90s.)

So I looked at the little red can that he was drinking from and said, "What is that thing that you're drinking right there? That's called a five-hour what?"

He said, "Five-hour energy drink. But this is *real* energy."

I said, "Oh, okay, because you can see the can and taste the liquid, it's real energy." He agreed with that, so I said, "Okay, cool." Then I talked about energy with the entire group for the next two hours. At that point, I was totally inspired to do so.

Ten years later, my students in mid-2005, 2006 are begging for discussions on energy, so much so that we had to make it a main part of our NLP trainings. By 2016, we were opening with discussions on energy, and people get it.

One of my favorite sayings is "Water is wet, the sky is blue, energy is real, and it affects you too," and that's true whether you believe in it or not. Thank God energy believes in *you* because energy has not only been scientifically proven to affect your body, it is the factor that affects your cells and your genetic expression the most.

I could go down a rabbit hole of epigenetics, citing Bruce Lipton's work on energy and environment, and Deepak Chopra's work on mindfulness-based meditation. For the purpose of this book though, I want to just keep it simple. What is energy? Why is it so important, and what role does it play in hoʻoponopono?

The answer is really straightforward. Energy is the gas in a gas tank. It's different than motivation. Motivation is a specific emotional response. Emotions are energy. As Tris Thorp says, "E-motions are energy in motion."

Just because you can't see energy doesn't mean it's not real. If you go with the idea that energy isn't real because you can't see it, then you also have to say that emotions aren't real because you can't see them, and your mind isn't real because you can't see it either, and electricity isn't real, and neither is air or oxygen. In other words, all of these things aren't real, or all of them are.

You cannot sit reading this and argue, "Well, oxygen is real, and my thoughts are real, and my emotions are real. But energy isn't."

I'd rather have you say, "I don't get it. I need to understand what energy is." All you really need to understand comes from your own experience. You can't see your emotions, but you can experience the effects of your emotions. You can't see your thoughts, but you can definitely experience the effects of thoughts.

I can't see oxygen, but as I'm writing this book and looking out my window, it's a windy day here in Hawaiʻi. I can see the leaves moving. So I'm going to trust that wind is blowing even though I can't see the wind. I know the wind exists, even though it's invisible to my eye, because I can see the effects of it.

We can all see the effects of energy. Have you ever awakened on a day with a million things to do? You have an endless laundry list.

The plan the night before was to get to bed early. You did. Everything was geared up. You're supposed to get a ton of work done that day. But when you wake up, you've got no gas in the gas tank. You're lying flat on your back, thinking, *Why did I schedule all of this today?*

You can barely get out of bed. You feel drained, like your battery is running low. You feel like you need to find a way to recharge. (Even those of us who act like energy doesn't exist still use the same terminology for it!)

You've also probably had the opposite experience where you have a day when you're not supposed to do anything. You're supposed to just chill out and relax. Your only goal for the day was to be calm and serene, yet you wake up like the Energizer Bunny on crack. (I'm talking about good crack, not bad crack.)

So you find yourself bouncing around the house— mopping the floor, painting the walls, mowing the grass, sanding that cabinet. You can't help but get a million things done, and you don't know where all of this energy came from.

That's the effects of energy. That's like seeing the breeze move the leaves. That's like feeling the emotional response. You see the effects of energy and witness what energy does. We know energy exists because we see the results from energy; that is the simplest way of understanding that energy exists. So to be really clear, if you can't see it, it doesn't mean that it doesn't exist. It means you can't see it.

To understand what energy is, you look at the *results* of energy or lack thereof. If we go to spiritual teachings, all spiritual teachings say that we're beings of light. That we have energy. That everything boils down to energy.

Physics actually says that the entire world around us is a physical expression of energy and that energy cannot be created or destroyed, just moved through three different experiences: creation, transformation, and completion. Any physicist will tell you—and this is physics, not quantum physics—that everything just boils down to energy. Quantum physics has actually brought us almost full circle to ancient spiritual teachings.

In the early days of science, scientists invented the microscope. They wanted to delve into physical structure and prove some of the ancient teachings, so they broke open a brick and opened up a piece of wood. They were expecting to see energy there through their microscopes because the ancient teachings said it was there. But they didn't.

Because of this, in some places, they destroyed ancient concepts and burned ancient libraries to the ground, all in the name of science. As scientists got better measuring devices, they found cells and crystals. They got even better measuring devices and found microbes and even tinier things. With even better measuring devices, they found atoms and claimed, "Wow. That's the tiniest thing that we could possibly find"—until they found subatomic particles. Then they found that there is way more space *in between* the nucleus and the subatomic particles then there are atoms.

And they created even better measuring devices, and scientists had to come up with a new terminology for what they could see. They called it "quantum." They found quarks and neutrinos. And lo and behold, they devised a better measuring device, and at the deepest level of everything, they found energy and condensed light. They found themselves right back at the beginning.

The ancients weren't being metaphorical. They were being literal. We are beings of energy. We are beings of light.

In the book *Biology of Belief*, Dr. Bruce Lipton talks about research that was done in the '80s that proves that energy affects your cells first and foremost. He maps the entire process out scientifically. Deepak Chopra talks about how scientists can measure a genetic shift in your genetic expression after an eight-hour mindfulness meditation. Pharmaceutical companies are now working with individuals like Deepak Chopra on bio-field energy.

Yale has recently done research using people like Huna energy workers, reiki masters, and chi gong masters. These researchers were able to measure energy coming out of a person's hand and measure the effect of the energy hitting another person, even while that person is looking away.

Science is now acknowledging that, at the deepest level of who we are from a quantum physics perspective, we have energy inside us. That energy affects our cells. That energy can accumulate and get stuck in the form of baggage, and that baggage can even be measured along neuropathways. In the book *Foundation Theory,* Dr. Paul Goodwin was able to measure baggage along neuropathways. His work was done in the late '80s, early '90s, yet very few people picked up on the importance of his findings.

Science is able to measure energy centers in the bodies, which ancient systems called "chakras." Around your body is a field that goes from the bottom of your pelvic bone to the top of your head and acts like a magnetic field, holding all your energy together. And it needs to be held together because it is powerful!

For example, you have tens of trillions of atoms in your body. One scientist told me we have close to 70 trillion. (I've never bothered to count.) If we took just one of those atoms out of your body and split it, the city you're sitting in right now would be blown to nothing—and you have tens of trillions of these in your body! You are a walking nuclear power plant, and that energy filters down through your thoughts and your emotions and affects your physical body. Part of the process of ho'oponopono is connecting with the energy that will heal your body and heal the emotional baggage to make forgiveness possible.

Positive and Negative Energy

Energy is just energy. You can use electricity to hurt someone, to shock them. You can use electricity to turn on a blender and make a shake. Energy is just energy. Yet we've all experienced both "negative" and "positive" energy.

Energy itself isn't negative, but you can have negative intentions with the energy. Even if you're not someone who is deeply in touch with your emotions, you've probably had an experience of walking into a family or a work situation and you immediately felt the tension. That's the result of energy. You've walked into an energy field that has less-than-happy experiences in it.

During the ho'oponopono process, we tap into a positive energy and use it to heal ourselves, to make ourselves pono. There are many ways to tap into this energy. For me, when my daughter looks at me, I stand in a light, and I know how much she loves me. There is no doubt there. There is no hesitation. I feel that strong positive energy.

A person who is religious or spiritual might experience this positive healing energy as being the presence of Spirit, in the presence of Source, in the presence of God. In that moment, it's as if nothing could go wrong. You hear or experience almost no negativity. You connect up with your spirit, your soul and your higher self.

For others, you might be in this energy when you're doing the thing you love to do, when You're in the zone and everything feels so right. Someone could march up to you and say the most awful thing, but you'd still just smile and think, *No worries. I'm good right now.* Or maybe you find that energy when you fall in love. The person you love looks at you, and you feel a glow inside that just melts everything else away. Even when you're having an awful day, your lover just gives you one look or a hug and all the problems of the day disappear. That's the level of energy you want to plug into during hoʻoponopono.

Maybe you find this positive energy at your favorite place. We all have a place we love, whether it's a vacation spot, or a restaurant, or maybe a place in nature. When you get there, you automatically feel a level of peace and calm. It's helpful to identify your own experience of that energetic quality because that's a quality we bring in for hoʻoponopono. We're looking to bring in an energy that allows you to feel healed.

In ancient Hawaiʻi, people who did energy work were people who tapped into some very specific types of energy that could then be moved or connected to other individuals. Essentially, in the hoʻoponopono process you yourself are connecting up with that energy.

Morrnah Simeona used to say that if you don't feel like you're ready to forgive as you're doing the process, you haven't healed yourself up enough with positive energy. If you stood in that light, if you stood in that positive energy, forgiveness would be possible. If you were having trouble, she would say to flow more energy— flow more energy to yourself and to the other person you're imagining doing this with. When you do that, forgiveness is possible.

When people use the term "flow energy" from a Huna perspective, I see it more as plugging in. Rather than thinking of flowing like a waterfall or like a faucet, think of it as if you're plugging in to an outlet above your head.

You're setting up a connection to it. When you plug in, that energy will instantaneously be in your body to allow you to feel completely healed and loved inside.

During the ho'oponopono process, you'll imagine that you have a Higher Source (in whatever form your belief system carries) and that you're plugging in to that. When you plug in to it, like plugging your computer in, the energy is instantly available.

We're plugging in to the energy that allows for healing to take place. So as you do this process, think of the times where you have stood in an energy that made you feel pono, where nothing could go wrong, where you were standing in that light.

The Aka Connection

Another part of ho'oponopono is disconnecting. The Hawaiians believed that energy needed to connect through a conduit, just like an electrical wire needs to have an insulation. When you have an extension cord where the copper is exposed, you know to throw it away because you don't want to be electrocuted. You can't see electricity passing through the copper, but you know you'll get zapped without the covering to protect you.

The Hawaiians believed in what they called *aka*, an aka cord or an aka connection. This is the umbilical cord between you and your Higher Self as well as between you and everyone around you. Everyone's experienced the aka connection. Have you ever been at home, thinking of someone, and suddenly they call you? They might even say, "For some reason, I was just thinking about you." Consciously or unconsciously, they were able to feel the energy of your thoughts about them.

Or maybe you've had the sudden urge to call someone, and they answer, saying, "I was just about to call you." Maybe you've had a moment where you knew who was about to call or knew your phone was about to ring. We think of it as an intuitive hit. Actually, it wasn't intuitive as much as it was the experience of energy coming in through the aka connection. You experienced energy flowing in, then you picked up on it and responded.

One of my favorite examples that I use in my trainings is walking through a crowded area and you feel like someone is staring at you. You turn, and you see that one person. There could be 100 people milling about, yet that person sticks out like a sore thumb. That's because energy flows where attention goes. When you focus in on someone who is hypersensitive to energy, they'll pick up on it instantly.

I dance hula and take Hawaiian cultural lessons from my teacher Kumu Etua Lopes, who wrote the forward to my book *The Foundation of Huna*. He talks about how we're connected with everyone.

Ho'oponopono with Those You Love

Part of the ho'oponopono process is to disconnect, and we'll talk about how that's done when we get into the specific steps of the process. But let's be really clear from the start: when you disconnect, if you're doing ho'oponopono because someone has *wronged* you, you disconnect from the negativity, from the baggage, *and* you can choose to disconnect from the person.

When you do hoʻoponopono and disconnect from someone that you love dearly, you do it with the intention of wanting to make a new connection. I want to see my kids grow up and become young adults. I don't want to hold them as being babies forever. Each time I do hoʻoponopono with them, I am releasing who my children have been and getting to form a fresh relationship with who they are right now.

Papa Bray talked about the fact that these connections can get built up with old residue—old gunk of how you used to be. I have a really good friend, an amazing woman, a powerhouse of a woman. Yet the moment she gets in front of her dad, she's daddy's little girl again. If you regress to an old behavior every time you're around a certain person, odds are good your aka connection has an old residue in it. The idea with hoʻoponopono is to cut that old connection with its residue. Then after you become pono, you can make a new connection.

A married woman in one of my trainings was concerned about doing this. She said, "I don't want to disconnect from my husband. We've been connected for twenty, thirty years. It will take that long to build up the connection again."

I said, "Oh, my goodness. That's twenty or thirty years of old behavior patterns and old energy."

When you disconnect with the intention of reconnecting with love, when you're pono in that moment and free of old baggage, that brand-new connection is stronger than your old, worn-out extension cord. When you do hoʻoponopono with someone you love, your intention is to reconnect and make a stronger new connection.

This isn't to say that your old connection is bad, just that it represents old residue of old energy—of old ways of being, doing, and having. By connecting with new energy by doing your release work, you now have the ability to reconnect and strengthen that bond. You'll probably even discover new, wonderful things about that person you love that you simply couldn't see before.

Hoʻoponopono with People in Your World

You form an aka connection with *everyone* you interact with, not just the people you love or those who have wronged you. Your co-workers, your clients, your students, the babysitter, your barber—you are connected to all of them. Because we're human, we tend to bump into others and step on one another's toes. We misunderstand and unintentionally hurt one another. Even in casual relationships, the aka connection can build up residue and strain communication.

When I first began teaching, I had a student who is a brilliant woman, an extremely intelligent medical doctor. During the training, she openly admitted that, because of the letters after her name, she felt that she knew more than I did. (I hadn't yet earned my doctorate.) I have to admit I was deeply offended. I said to her, "You're coming to this training to learn from me. This is my family lineage. This goes back twenty-eight generations into the Hawaiian culture. And because you have two letters after your name and I don't, you think you know more than I do?" She nodded. I said, "But you're not here for a medical conference. You're here for a Huna."

She said, "I know. That's my big issue."

I was in my twenties and had just started teaching, so you have to forgive me because I didn't do ho'oponopono that night. The moment I walked into the class the next day, I saw her standing there. I took one look at her and thought, "Ugh, she's still here."

Well, of course she was still there. She flew all the way out to the middle of the Pacific Ocean. She wasn't going to bail out on the training. She wanted to learn what I had to teach. She was honestly just expressing her issue to me. Just by being in her presence and feeling that connection with her, I instantly felt offended and defensive again. Sometimes we tie baggage to a specific person, and our energy connection ignites the baggage that we have that we haven't resolved. With this woman, even just thinking of her lit up my baggage.

Ho'oponopono resolved it. She actually became one of my long-term students and served as a board member for the university that I ran. She is an amazing, gifted woman. Thank God I did ho'oponopono and chose to re-establish a new connection. If I hadn't, I would have missed out on the great relationship we've had.

Ho'oponopono with Those Who Have Died

We've talked about ho'oponopono with those who have wronged you and those you love. The third type of person that you would do a ho'oponopono with is someone who has passed away.

Morrnah Simeona was an amazing teacher and well-known for her research and work with ho'oponopono. She taught Dr. Hew Len, who carries on her foundation. I heard a story about her last days when she was in the hospital. Some of her students were with her, and she told them to have everyone do ho'oponopono the moment she passed away to let her live on in their memories but disconnect from the physical body. She wanted them to allow her to disconnect from the empty vessel and allow her to transition.

This may sound tough, even impossible, if the loss is recent. When my daughter lost her friend, she wasn't ready to disconnect in the beginning. Morrnah Simeona and Papa Bray both said the cutting of the aka cord is optional and not required … but I highly recommend it.

I work with clients one-on-one, and I have taught probably close to 100,000 students at this point. I *always* recommend cutting the aka connection because it is in that moment where you free yourself from the baggage. It is in that moment where you wipe the slate clean with your loved ones and can reconnect. It's in that moment where you can disconnect from someone who has passed away and let them live on in your memories.

To do that, you need to stand in the light. As I've said, part of the ho'oponopono process involves your imagining a higher source of energy above you, whatever you believe is the higher source. If you're religious, that could be God. If you're spiritual, it could be Higher Self, or *aumakua* in Hawaiian. If you're very scientific, it could just be quantum energy or it could be universal energy. It can be whatever you want.

In the process, you allow that energy to come in. When you stand in that energy and when you stand in that light, it frees up the path for you to gain forgiveness.

I ask my groups sometimes, "Have you ever had a spiritual experience?" Almost everyone says they do, so I say, "Great. In that moment, is it possible for anything to go wrong?" They usually say it's not possible, and I say, "Great. That's the energy we're connecting with."

All things being equal, nothing can go wrong in that energy. When you stand in that light from Higher Self, forgiveness becomes possible. That is really the most important thing you need to know about energy. In my upcoming book about Energy and Mana, the whole book will be on energy, not just crammed into one measly, little chapter. For our purposes here, I don't want to overcomplicate it.

(*For more information on energy and the part it plays in your life, please see the Resources Section at the end of this book.*)

6

Background of Hoʻoponopono

I tell a story in my book *The Foundation of Huna* about seeing my dad meditating when I was five. In the spirit of total transparency, when my mom explained to me that he was meditating and blocking out all distractions, my first thought was to sneak into the room and jump on the waterbed to shoot him into the ceiling like Wile E. Coyote and the Road Runner.

When my attempt failed, I 'fessed up to my mom and (after my punishment ended), I asked her again, "What was Dad doing?" She explained about meditation to me, and I began to meditate.

Meditation transformed my life because as a kid, I had so much energy. Oh, my goodness. When the bell rang for recess, I'd bolt out the door. I'd run around the playground and climb up the slide—not by the stairs but on the slide itself because it took longer and more energy.

Then I'd swing. In my mind, I'd imagine the swing going all the way around—360 degrees. I did whatever I could to expend all that energy, and yes, I was a sweaty, stinky mess. But at least when I got back to class, I could sit still. My teacher hated it when I bounced.

But then my mom taught me to meditate as a five-year-old. When I meditated, I could suddenly calm myself without having to run. Even though I didn't know what energy was at that point, meditation opened up my spiritual path.

I meditated consistently as a kid. During that time, David "Papa" Bray Jr. (the son of one of the last practicing Kahuna, David "Daddy" Bray) instructed my father, Tad James, in his family's system of Huna. Papa Bray wanted to share this information with someone to preserve the lineage because he had no one in his own family who was interested in learning the material at the time. So in the late 1980s, he gave my father permission to learn, practice, and teach the Huna of the Bray family. My family was charged with carrying on the lineage.

When I was about twelve years old, my dad sat me down and taught me a meditation based on Hawaiian culture. I learned ho'oponopono at the kitchen table, and we talked about energy. It opened up my mind. It opened up my life. It made sense to me.

When I started teaching weekend trainings in my twenties and then began teaching at our Huna workshop, I felt my spirit awaken. I felt a deep desire to not just add credibility to this field, but to share this with as many people as I possibly could. Interestingly enough, at the same time that I began my path to become a doctor of psychology, I also began my path as *Kumu* (teacher). Uncle George gave me the title "Kumu" in 2006, and I began teaching the Huna workshops as the main teacher. Since my first trainings in the '90s, I've witnessed a shift and expansion in our students' consciousness collectively and individually.

After becoming a doctor and studying ho'oponopono, the thing that I treasure the most is my lineage. I appreciate the fact that my father studied directly with someone who was the son of one of the last practicing Kahunas in ancient Hawai'i, who claimed a twenty-five-generation lineage going all the way back into the ancient culture. Depending on which chant you listen to, depending on how you date it and what school of Hawaiian studies it comes from, you could look at the Hawaiian practices as going back a few thousand years. Uncle George even once said that they go back tens of thousands of years. I've heard archaeologists say that's not possible, yet dinosaurs didn't exist until we found them, so who knows ...

Maybe it was ten thousand years or maybe just a few thousand. What I know is that ho'oponopono has always been a major part of the Hawaiian culture. *Malamapono* is a Hawaiian saying. "Malama" means to cherish. "Pono" is the state of well-being we've been talking about.

My lineage goes back twenty-eight generations into Hawaiian culture when you count Papa Bray, my dad, and me. And I *malama* that. I cherish that. My son, Ethan, who began hearing about this as a kid, has done energy work with me. He took his first Huna training as a ten-year-old, and at the age of sixteen, he began to teach at our workshops to the upper levels of Huna. Ethan is carrying on this family lineage, as is my daughter who has attended the workshops and learns about energy from me at the kitchen table.

So ho'oponopono isn't something that I learned in a book or learned at a weekend seminar. It's a practice that is a part of my family. In ancient time in Hawai'i, certain families carried certain teachings.

I was blessed to have the opportunity to teach at the University of Hawai'i, Hawaiian Studies Program. I was brought in not because I'm a doctor, not because I studied ho'oponopono, but because of my lineage and who I've had the privilege to study with. The study of this material never ends. Well-respected teachers like George Na'ope and John Ka'imikaua still study to this day with Kumu Etua Lopes.

My point in sharing this with you is that these teachings go back into ancient times. The Hawaiians believed that forgiveness wasn't an option. It was a requirement. I can say that to you with congruence, that in every situation, no matter what occurs, you are required to forgive.

The Three Wrongs

The Hawaiians have a really easy way of summarizing what required forgiving. There were only three things you could do wrong in the Hawaiian culture. They were *hala*, *hewa*, and *'ino*.

Hala is to miss the path. For example, a student raises his hand and asks me a question. I'm five minutes into the explanation when I look at him and ask, "Does that make sense?"

He says, "Yeah. That's awesome. But it's not what I was asking." I obviously wasn't paying attention. That's a hala. I missed the path.

We've all missed the path at some time or other. Maybe we zoned out and burned the steaks on the grill. Maybe we didn't read the washing instructions on our partner's shirt and we shrank it. Maybe we forgot someone's birthday—or our own anniversary! All of these would be considered hala.

Hewa is to go overboard, like in the training where I was so motivated that one student thought I was aggressive. That's hewa—to go overboard, to go to excess. Think of conversations where one person talks so much that no one else can get a word in, or being at a little kids' soccer game where a parent is so excited that she runs up and down the field yelling out instructions to her child. That's hewa.

ʻIno is where you have some intent to do harm. Maybe you're upset at your significant other and think, *Tonight, we're going out to dinner. Five nights ago, she ignored me, and tonight's important to her. So I'll ignore her and teach her a lesson.* We've probably all done that— held back something or withheld affection like you're God in their universe and it's your turn to teach them something valuable because you know so much better than they do. That's an ʻino—along with things like murder, robbery and assault. Anything you do, big or small, that has the intent to cause hurt is an ʻino.

In all of these instances, forgiveness is required for the other person because we've done them all. No one is perfect. No one. You can be a Kumu. You can be a doctor of psychology, a master trainer of NLP, and you still sometimes miss the path. You still sometimes go overboard. You still sometimes think that it's your job to give someone else a lesson. It's not. When someone does a wrong to you, if you ever want to be forgiven, you have to first give forgiveness.

Self-Forgiveness

In ancient Hawai'i it was believed that in each of these instances, there were opportunities for you to become more forgiving of yourself by forgiving others. In the process of ho'oponopono, I get asked so often, "Can I do this with myself?"

The thing is, that's not how we experience life or reality. We experience who we are through our interactions with other individuals. We notice our hala, our missing the path, our hewa, going overboard by others' reactions. We experience our 'ino, intentional harm, through the experience of other individuals.

Maybe as a parent, you have had to scold your kid for an extended period of time. Maybe you've had a rough moment or two with a loved one. When you get back in their presence, you can almost see their response to you. That's when you realize that you may need to forgive and be forgiven.

For instance, I experience this with my students. Sometimes as a Kumu, I have to find a balance between helping people on their path and respecting the ancient culture. I remember one student with whom I had to have a very direct conversation who was doing things that, from a Hawaiian perspective, would not be pono.

While I didn't intend for the discussion to be offensive, the person was slightly offended. When I finished what I needed to say, I knew that things were not yet right, but I knew they could become right and that I had said enough. So, I stopped. I looked at her and said, "Okay, I think I've made my point. Let's just sit with this for a little bit and see how it goes."

A day later, she came back in front of me. The moment she walked in the room, you could see that her demeanor had changed. She was walking and talking with someone, and then she glanced up and saw me. She took a deep breath, and her head dropped a little bit.

I thought, *Okay. What's the big lesson here?* The lesson was that I had maybe gone overboard explaining something. Now when she came into my presence, she picked up on that energy, on what had occurred before.

I felt I had an opportunity to make this right. I felt that maybe from her perspective, I had said too much. Maybe if I had said just a little bit less, maybe she would have absorbed it. I wanted to forgive myself because I was beating myself up, but in actuality, I didn't *know* to beat myself up until I had that experience with her—that interaction.

I was taught this as I was guided and mentored by Uncle George. He said that your awareness of your wrong comes through another person, and when you do ho'oponopono, your forgiveness comes through that other person as well. You learned that you had gone overboard because of your interaction with the other person, so you do ho'oponopono with them (personally or in your mind), not just yourself.

In ho'oponopono, the word *pono* is repeated twice. *Ho'o* means "to make." The word *pono* twice means "with yourself and others."

By doing ho'oponopono with my student, it actually allowed me to forgive myself. When I approached her to do face-to-face ho'oponopono, it made things right between the two of us. During our discussion, she asked me for forgiveness too. She believed she had overreacted and her demeanor that day was not anger towards me, it was embarrassment of taking the experience into the negative. We both laughed, hugged and were able to imua (move forward).

Ho'oponopono is done with other people, and by doing that, we become pono with ourselves. There's a different process that you do to release baggage with yourself. But you can't cut the cord with yourself, and you can't disconnect in the way you disconnect with someone through ho'oponopono.

Starting a New Path

In ancient times, you were required to do ho'oponopono whenever you were embarking on a new path because you wanted to start off a new path pono. When it was my turn to teach Huna, when it was my turn to become Kumu, and before I taught my first class as Kumu, I went to Hilo and met with Uncle George because he was the person who would give me permission and make me a Kumu. When I got there, part of what we did was become pono with each other.

He had to become pono with what I knew, so I was quizzed. He had to become pono with things that had happened in the past. He asked me questions about why certain things were a certain way. He wanted to know how was I sharing it with my son, my daughter? He wanted to know how I was setting it up so that these teachings lived on.

Before he could say, "Okay, you are a Kumu now," he needed to be pono with me and my path. Then he helped me to become pono with things that had happened in the past because, when you start a new path with baggage, you're doomed to experience that baggage, dragging the baggage with you.

For example, think about starting a new relationship. If you ended the prior relationship with a lot of anger and blame, odds are good that you'll carry that baggage forward into the next relationship. Whatever you *didn't* learn from the past, you're going to have to get that lesson with the next person. But if you end your former relationship and become pono with it, you start with a clean slate.

In the ancient Hawaiian culture, it was believed you should start off new paths pono, being right with yourself and any old stuff that had happened. When you did, then you didn't drag any of that old energy into the new path. However, if you don't get pono, if you start a new path with anger or blame or hurt, that anger, blame, or hurt becomes a part of the new path and a part of the new experience. You're either doomed to re-experience it, or it becomes a major theme in the new path that you cannot overcome.

I'm a big fan of becoming pono before starting a path, not just because it feels right, not just because it is how the Hawaiians did it for centuries, but because it makes sense. Wipe the slate clean before starting new. Clean out your closet before buying new clothes. Clean out the garage before putting stuff in there. It makes sense to wash your clothes before you put them on. You don't put on dirty clothes.

Yet so many of us start a new path wearing our dirty old clothes instead of being free of the baggage and starting something new and clean. Think of ho'oponopono as a means of wiping the slate clean with yourself and others, being free of the baggage, stepping into a new energy and into your light. It's freeing yourself to move forward and experience third grade instead of repeating second grade over and over again.

Which Tool to Use?

Ho'oponopono is not a fix-everything technique. It's one tool. If the only screwdriver you have is a Phillips-head screwdriver, and the screw that you need to tighten is a flat-head, well, you're screwed. Many people write books as if this one tool fixes everything. It's true that I can get a screw into a piece of wood with a hammer, but it rips the wood apart.

Ho'oponopono is just one tool. Sometimes you need a screwdriver. Sometimes you need a hammer. It all depends on the situation.

There are four major techniques that I teach throughout my trainings to help people release their baggage and move through their self-imposed obstacles. Ho‘oponopono is one of them because we sometimes tie our baggage to other people, connecting our issues to an individual.

For example, my daughter hit a rough patch in the fourth grade. Skylar has such a big heart. She loves so much of her life and really loves to have beauty and joy and happiness around her. And part of how much she loves life includes wanting to have other people be happy around her and wanting other people to have joy around her.

Being nine was tough for her. Certain friends went from being her friend to suddenly not being a friend anymore. That can hurt. We used ho‘oponopono in that case because her issue was related to a person.

When I was a kid, I had a friend who went from being my best friend to joining about ten other guys who jumped me, threw me off a bike, and beat the tar out of me. He had been my best friend the year before, then suddenly, he was with the popular kids. And the popular kids said, "Let's beat the heck out of the white guy." Ho‘oponopono is for that.

Another major tool I teach is called *ho‘oku‘u*. Ho‘oku‘u, which means "to make something release," is for releasing anger, sadness, fear, or guilt—just general negative emotions.

In the NLP (neuro linguistics programming) trainings, I take a more psychological approach, and we call that process Mental and Emotional Release® (MER). In my book *Mental and Emotional Release®*, we talk about the MER process and how it works to free people of their baggage.

Parts Integration is another tool I teach in the NLP trainings. Parts Integration is used when you're tugged in two different directions, like when a part of you wants to do something but another part of you wants to do something different. Another great tool is Prime Concerns, which is an energy-release technique I teach at Master Practitioner level in the NLP trainings. Prime Concerns is about dealing with the Shadow on a surface level. Because working with the Shadow is so important, I wrote a book dedicated to the Shadow called *Integrate the Shadow*.

I mention all of this because our baggage can show up in different ways and requires different tools.

Ho'oponopono is for baggage related to another individual or group of people. For example, if your dad kept telling you over and over again how ugly you are and you grew up with a negative self-image, you want to heal your self-image. But it came from your dad, so you do ho'oponopono with your dad. If you just developed a poor self-image on your own and you've got a ton of baggage inside, then you'd use a release technique like MER.

A lot of people talk about self-forgiveness, but I think more in terms of "release" for the baggage that is just about you. Maybe you feel disappointed in yourself for not living up to your potential, or you're angry at yourself for not studying as well as you could have, or maybe you feel sad that you haven't pursued your dream or made the effort to find the love of your life. In a sense, what you want is not self-forgiveness. Dealing with those issues probably needs self-integration or some form of release work.

(*To learn more about Huna, please see the Resources Section at the end of this book.*)

7

The Process of Hoʻoponopono

I'm guessing that some people who picked up this book have skipped everything else and jumped right to this chapter! We're finally getting to the point, right? Well, if you've had an experience of hoʻoponopono or a similar forgiveness process, this chapter will make sense.

If you *haven't* had an experience of it, you may be missing some critical information. (You know, simple things like who to do this with and what energy is …) I've covered some basics and the foundation in previous chapters, breaking down concepts like baggage and the part that energy plays. If you've jumped all the way to this chapter just to see the process, that's great. I'd just respectfully request that you read the other chapters so that we have a shared understanding of things like energy and baggage.

When I was eighteen, I moved out of the house and got a job delivering pizzas, which was one of the best jobs

I ever got. The reason I liked it so much is that pizza is a food made by God. You take it to someone's house, and they pay you, plus give you extra money. I loved delivering pizzas!

Unfortunately, my car couldn't make it to the top of the hill where the people who have lots of money lived, so I set a goal. And a few months later, I was an assistant manager. Three months after that, I was a manager, running the pizza restaurant, making enough money. I had a brand-new car.

I told the guy who promoted me, "I'm eighteen. I don't know what the hell I'm doing." (Again, I sometimes have no filter.) I'm always very, very honest.

He said to me, "You have the gift of communication." (That came from my background in neuro linguistic programming.) He continued, "You're always so calm." (That came from Huna, and energy, and ho'oponopono—but I refused to talk about it.)

I fell asleep during that period of my life. I disappeared. I got into the working mode, what Dr. Arjuna Ardagh called "the Iago trance." He wrote, "The Iago trance is a state that we've really come to accept as normal, even if we may not feel it to be natural."

The Iago trance is where you get up in the morning. You work out. You get the kids up. You make them breakfast. You take them to school. You go to work. You pick them up. You pay the bills. You cook dinner. You watch TV. You go to sleep. You get up. You work out. You wake the kids up. You cook them breakfast. You get them ready for school. You drop them off. You go to work. You pick them up. You come home. You pay the bills. You cook dinner. You watch TV. You go to sleep.

I went into that trance as an eighteen-year-old for just over two years. I finally woke up from that trance as a twenty-year-old, after being offered a full-time position in a department store where they were going to pay for my college because of my gift of communication.

I freaked out. I quit. I quit the job because I realized there's more to life than running a department store. If you happen to run a department store, my hat goes off to you. I think it's an amazing thing. But it isn't who I am.

I wasn't pono with who I was. I asked my father if I could come back and work for his company. He looked at me and said, "First, I need you to remember who you are." He sent me to Kona to live with Uncle George for a summer. (He actually said I had to go until I "figured it out." I defiantly had some fear and uncertainty.)

So I went. I had met Uncle George when I was five or six, and he remembered me, even though *I* had forgotten who I was. Many of us do.

I was so angry with myself at that time because after meditating at five and doing NLP as an eleven-year-old, walking on fire with Tony Robbins as an eleven-year-old, doing ho'oponopono and energy work with my dad as a teenager, I'd been acting like none of it existed. For almost three years, I lived in the world of get up, pay your bills, go to school, blah, blah, blah. I was so pissed off with myself.

I showed up in Kailua-Kona and Uncle George was the sweetest, most amazing individual. He said, "I have so many things to share with you and teach you, yet I can't put anything into you right now." My dad used to say, "Sometimes when you're teaching someone, you have to look at the student. And if their cup is full, there is nothing else you can pour into it."

So Uncle George took me to Honaunau, which is a place for release. We walked into the park that Hawaiians have used for thousands of years to help people let go of their stuff.

Uncle George talked to me about the fact that you have to accept and sometimes surrender to your path. He told me about how he had created the Merrie Monarch Hula Festival. As a Hawaiian, other Hawaiians would walk up to him and say, "What the hell is wrong with you? You should let these old ways die." He told me that at the first Merrie Monarch Hula Festival, they had to give seats away. They had to beg people to come to it because it was so opposite of how people were thinking at the time.

He teared up and said, "My own people turned against me." Then he said to me, "There are times in life when things don't make sense. And there are times in life when you'll question. That's natural. When you're pono, when you're right with who you are, you're able to move forward on the path. You're able to hold to that tiny little piece of fire that's still burning in the rain as the one thing that is going to keep you warm."

Uncle George helped me through a bunch of release work that I needed to do. When his top student, Etua (who teaches hula at The Palace on the big island of Hawaiʻi), decided to enter the fiftieth anniversary of the Merrie Monarch Hula Festival in 2013, I got to drum and chant on that stage with him. I have studied with him since 2002, and to this day I learn something new in every class.

I remember thinking back to the fact that Uncle George had to start that path fighting his own people, trying to make this thing live and having to be pono because in the Hawaiian culture, hoʻoponopono was treated as sacred.

Not an Instant Cure

Morrnah Simeona used to teach the actual process of hoʻoponopono. Her student, Dr. Hew Len, originally did too; however, he began to teach what has become known as the hoʻoponopono prayer instead (where you say four things and you're done). Dr. Hew Len, Joe Vitale, and even Tony Robbins teach that prayer in their own classes. The prayer is beautiful, but if saying four things fixed everything, this book would have ended in the first paragraph.

I could have written, "Just say happy thoughts, and everything will be fine." I think we're more evolved than that, and teachers who tell you to just say happy things and everything will be okay may be doing you a disservice.

What I'm sharing with you is the process that I was taught and taken through by my father and by Uncle George, and it is the process that I continue to teach. Others don't teach it anymore, maybe because they think that people who live in Western society can't handle the details. Maybe the alternative is faster to explain, or maybe it's just easier to teach.

The prayer was developed based on the major steps in the process, so you will recognize it there; however, it goes deeper.

I don't know their reasons for switching to and/or just teaching the prayer, and personally, I think many people in Western society can handle the details. What they can't handle is the responsibility—the responsibility to *do this every day* and *for every situation*.

So again, this is the original process as taught to me when I was a kid. In ancient times, ho'oponopono was done in one of three ways.

The first way was face-to-face. You've got a grudge with the person, so it's time to release that grudge and deal with your garbage around it.

The second way was to do the entire thing in your head. You closed your eyes. You dealt with your own stuff. You realized that everyone was just a reflection of you anyway, so you dealt with it in your head.

The third way was a combination of the two because in the face-to-face, you were not allowed to be aggressive. You were not allowed to bring intensity.

At the time that I'm writing this book, Ethan, my son, is a teenager and recently went through some rough things, as all teenagers do. I had to have a talk with him and help him become pono with himself. Before I did, I had to clear my own stuff out because I wanted to help him, not browbeat him. You don't want to do a pono meeting with someone if you have intensity.

This third way of doing hoʻoponopono is to first do it in your mind, as in the process I'm about to share with you. Only then do you go and talk to the person because when you talk to them, you can't be in blamer mode, and you can't be in pissed-off mode.

The process I'll share with you is the ancient approach, and it draws on a whole bunch of various concepts that we've already talked about. I'm going to share with you how to do this with one person. You can begin to practice it every single day of your life, like I do, with the people who have wronged you, with the people you love, and with the people who have passed away. I have recordings of classes where I have taught this in more detail, and I have recordings to help guide you through the process as well.

The Hoʻoponopono Process

Decide who you are going to do the process with— someone that has wronged you, someone you love, or someone that is no longer with you.

The first thing you need to do is create a quiet, calm space for yourself. I do hoʻoponopono in every scenario you can think of. I travel the world. I've taught on four continents. I've done hoʻoponopono on an airplane, in a subway, in the shower— you name it.

The first time you do this, you want to control your environment a little bit, so turn off your phone. Clear the area. If you love to have background music on to help calm you, put it on. In the back of my recordings, you'll hear music that I play to help people chill out, to relax a little bit.

Next, close your eyes and do some deep breathing. Breath in through the nose, and exhale through the mouth, making a gentle sound, "HA." Lengthen your exhale until it is about twice as long as your inhale.

With Uncle George, before we do a performance, we do deep breathing and make that gentle "HA" sound a few times. But with something important where you're building up energy, you might do this deep breathing for five or ten minutes. Do deep breathing and relaxation, maybe even meditation, until you get to a point where you feel very calm. You want to begin the process of ho'oponopono in a calm state.

Next, with your eyes still closed, imagine a stage below you and in front of you, kind of like a platform. Later, you will bring the individual you're doing the process for out onto this stage or platform.

As you create this platform, just allow your mind and your focus to come to what it is that you're doing. Next, imagine that directly above your head is a source of positive energy. It is your source of love, healing energy. In the chapter on energy, remember we talked about connecting with a moment where you felt total peacefulness? Now is the time to connect with that energy.

Allow loving, healing energy to connect to the top of your head. Like a gentle rainfall, like a waterfall, let it flow down into you, filling up your feet, your lower legs, your upper legs, up to your waist, filling up your torso, flowing down into both of your arms, filling up your neck, your head. Take whatever time you need to allow this energy to flow down into you and heal you completely.

The idea is that, when you are healed completely, forgiveness will be possible. During the process, continue to flow this energy, to let it just gently come down inside you and fill you up.

Now, you will invite the person out onto the stage that you want to engage in the process. It might be a person who has wronged you, a loved one with whom you want to strengthen your connection, or someone who's passed away. Bring that one person out onto the stage, and before you do anything else, at this moment, just open up your heart and—with love—flow energy down onto the stage. Imagine that it flows out of your heart down into the top of the other person's head to heal them the way that you were healed, completely inside and out.

When the other person is healed and you're healed completely, forgiveness is possible. Before that, it's not. So the key here is to really focus on healing yourself and healing the person on the stage.

Once complete healing has occurred, the discussion can begin. First, you tell the person on the stage, "I forgive you." You give the forgiveness from your heart with love and send it down to the stage into that person. The truer and more authentic you are with the gift of forgiveness, the more powerful this process will be. So you say to them, "I forgive you," and then you say,

"Please forgive me, too." This is where you get the forgiveness back.

Morrnah Simeona was once asked, "What if the person on the stage doesn't forgive you?" She said, "Well, it's in your head, and you should remember that you have control over the voices in your head." Then she continued, "Heal them up more. Heal them up more." If you were healed and they were healed, forgiveness would be possible.

After you say, "I forgive you. Please forgive me, too," you can say anything else you need to say to the person on the stage so that you can gain forgiveness. This is where you bear your soul … but you've got to watch your intensity. You are not allowed to bring emotional intensity to it.

Once you have expressed yourself, allow the other person the space to express himself or herself to you. When that is complete, thank the other person for being on the stage and thank them for being in your life. Thank them for the lessons they have given you, the seeds of learning, the ano'ai.

Next, imagine that there is a connection, the aka connection, between you and the person on stage. Imagine a blade that comes out of the energy from above and just gently floats down and cuts the connection between you and that person. As soon as it cuts that connection, let the person on stage fade away and disappear. Let the remaining connection dissolve back to energy, leaving you pono and free of the baggage.

Finally, give yourself sometime to reflect and connect with the feeling of being pono. If this was done with someone you love for the purpose of strengthening your connection, spend the time to reconnect with them. Call them, hug them, or just think about them.

Summary of the Ho‘oponopono Process

So here is an overview or summary of the ho‘oponopono process:

1. Decide who you are going to do the process with.
2. Create the appropriate space/environment for the process.
3. Start with some deep breathing to set the energy and intention.
4. Create a stage in your mind that is below you and in front of you.
5. Heal yourself with love, healing energy from your Higher Source.
6. Invite the person onto the stage.
7. Heal them from your heart to allow forgiveness to be possible.
8. Give and receive forgiveness. Say, "I forgive you, please forgive me."
9. Have any discussion you need to have to facilitate forgiveness.
10. Thank them for being on the stage and in your life.
11. Cut the aka connection, if it is appropriate to do so.
12. Allow time for you to experience the feeling of being pono.

Notes to the Ho'oponopono Process

When someone isn't feeling like the process has been effective, the issue is often the energy. It's critical that you remember a time where you stepped into the space of positive energy, of connection, of how amazing things can be and flow that same energy. Doing the process just as a visual without that energy will not have the same impact at all.

The second place where people tend to stumble is when they're healing the other person because they don't fully heal them. They're still holding a little bit of that grudge. Ho'oponopono releases the grudge, and you can't shortcut this part of the process if you want that release. You've got to heal the person you've called onto the stage.

Now once that's done, the next potential sticking point is where you say to the person, "Please forgive me, too," and that person says, "No." In my research, that's where I got some pushback. Some of those who went through the process said, "Oh, the person on the stage said 'no'." If that happens to you, you need to explore it. Take the time to really question whether or not you are ready to let it go. If you are, and you heal yourself and you heal that person, forgiveness would have to be possible. You've got to be ready for this. If you're ready for it and you're healed and they're healed, forgiveness is a done deal.

Finally, I sometimes see resistance to the cutting of the cords, the aka connection. People will say, "Oh, my daughter's nine. I can't cut the cord. She still needs my energy." That's ego. Your nine-year-old girl doesn't need your energy. She needs *her* energy. She needs to be able to stand on her own.

I had a student in L.A. who was a mother. She came up to me and said, "I was told, 'Don't disconnect from your kids.'"

I said, "Great. How old's your kid?"

She replied, "Twenty."

And I said, "Cut the cord!"

Think about it. When the baby's pulled out of the mom, how quickly do they cut the umbilical cord? Do they wait? Do they think about it? Do they go, "Oh my God"? No, they cut that thing as quickly as they can.

As I write this book, my daughter is nine, and she needs to be able to stand on her own. That's tough as a parent because you changed her diapers, and you dressed her, and you braided her hair. You think you're responsible for her. She's going to be a woman someday, though. How long you hold her back is how long it will take her to step into that power. You have to be willing to let go.

Skylar was born at the end of October in 2006. After being home with her for five days, I was thinking, "Good grief, we've got an NLP master practitioner training coming up, and I have not slept." November 1, 2006, I flew over to Kona and taught a training, and for the first time in a week, I got a full night's sleep. I felt so crazy good and fully rested.

Then I flew back to Honolulu, and she kept me up all night. I was grumpy. She was an infant. I did ho'oponopono with her. I had to forgive her because I was used to sleeping again. I can't complain about my girl because, after two weeks home, she started sleeping eight hours a night.

But the first two weeks were hell. I remember that day I came home, after having slept for two or three nights in a row. We were in an apartment, and Skylar's mother was exhausted. So I took Skylar out to the couch and stared at her while she was screaming at me in the middle of the night.

I remember looking at her and thinking, "Shut up!" She finally went back to sleep, and I put her in the crib. I did ho'oponopono so fast, you would not believe it. I was thinking, "This is the first girl born in my family for 400 years. I've got to love this girl, even though I want to strangle her right now." Even as an infant, I cut the aka connection with her. I already had built up some gunk in the line.

But another time when Skylar was about a year old, I went to California for six weeks. I missed her so much that occasionally I didn't cut the aka connection. Your decision to cut is situational, but if you're refusing to cut the connection because you think they need you, that's your ego. Read my book on ego and the conscious mind called *Find Your Purpose, Master Your Path*.

If you follow the steps and guidelines above, this process will be amazing for you. Diane experienced a true transformation after being assaulted and abused. One time through ho'oponopono changed her life because she was willing to let go of the old and embrace the new. Skylar was able to move on after her friend's death, though it took a few times through the process for her to be completely healed.

(For more information about the process of hoʻoponopono and to receive a recording to guide you through the process, please go to the Resources Section at the end of this book.)

8

Life as a Spiritual Practice

John Kaʻimikaua, one of my spiritual teachers, taught me some valuable lessons about making everything that you do a spiritual act. When my father taught the first Huna workshop in Kona in 1989, John was at that training along with Uncle George Naʻope and a whole bunch of Hawaiian spiritual teachers. John or his wife attended every single Huna workshop until he passed away in 2006.

John taught me that being spiritual, being connected with energy and being on your path, doesn't mean that you get everything right. It doesn't mean that you're perfect. It doesn't mean that you know everything. It means that you have a practice. It means that you're doing something on a *regular* basis.

If there's anything that I wish that I emphasized more in my book about Huna, it's the importance of a practice, of doing something regularly in order to improve your connection with yourself, with others, with energy, with mind-set. There are some basic principles that I think would be helpful for you as an individual to become more empowered. For a person to be healthy, they've got to do some form of exercise every day and they've got to eat right every day—not just on Sundays.

So the Hawaiians transcended the idea that you only have a physical body. The ancient Hawaiians understood that you have a spiritual body and you also have a mental body, an emotional body, and a physical body. (If you're uncomfortable with the term "spiritual," you can substitute "energy" for "spiritual.") So you have an energy body. You have a mind body. You have an emotional body, and you have a physical body.

You can't eat one salad and be healthy. You can't do just one session of release work and be done for ever after. You can't say, "I had a positive thought yesterday. I'm good." You can't think, "Oh, I felt energy yesterday. I'm okay." If you really want to enhance your life, you need a regular practice.

My daily practice comes from the idea that what you do on a regular basis becomes who you are. Aristotle said, "We are what we repeatedly do. Excellence, then, is not an act, but a habit." The idea that what we do over and over again sinks into who we are makes perfect sense.

I'll share my practice as an example of what might work for you. My daily practice in the morning is first to calm the energy down and wake up. I avoid Facebook, e-mails, text messages, and any other type of "outside" distraction. I focus on feeling the energy of what I want to do that day, the energy of creation. I'm creating my day. I'm putting the sunlight into my day. What intention do I want today? I set an intention every single morning.

If I'm in a rush, like going on vacation, and my flight's at 6:00 a.m., and I've got to wake up at three thirty so that I can wake my kids up in time to get to the airport, I give myself a break and condense the process. But I still give myself three seconds to set my intention for the day, which tells the energy how to behave and what I want from it. I tell the energy, "Here's how I need you to be. I need you to be calm. We're going to go see the TSA agents again today. We're going to fly to Honolulu. We're going to fly to California. Malie, be calm." Every morning, no matter what's going on, I set an intention. That's my number one suggestion.

My next big recommendation is gratitude. A daily practice of gratitude is where you are truly grateful for something—not just a surface-level gratitude. Why are you grateful? When you're able to express it and share it and go deep into your gratitude, it is powerful.

When I teach, I get to travel and see the world, and I love that my hotel rooms are so quiet. Then I come home to my daughter, who has a motor attached to her mouth. As I'm writing this, she's sitting in the room right now.

When I was in preschool, my teacher said, "I have a nickname for you, Matt. It's 'motor mouth.'"

I went home and told my mom proudly, "Mom, I have a nickname, 'motor mouth.'"

And she said, "Oh, honey, let's talk." I thought it was good, but my mom explained that my teacher may be a little bit tired of the fact that my mouth goes nonstop. Thank God I'm a teacher because if I wasn't, I don't know what I'd do with this mouth.

So when my daughter came home from preschool and said that her teacher called her a motor mouth, I was so proud. Her mother was not. But I was. I was proud in that moment.

I have to admit I love silence. When I'm on the road and in a hotel room, everything's quiet. When I come home, my daughter talks and I talk. And it takes me three seconds to look at her and think, "I am so thankful. I am so grateful."

Gratitude comes from forgiveness, and my daily practice includes forgiveness. Every night before I got to bed, I do ho'oponopono with anyone who has wronged me. If I think that I need to reconnect with a loved one— my love, my son, my daughter, my mom, my dad—I do ho'oponopono so that I can wake up the next morning and reconnect with them in a positive way. The process allows me to let go of the old patterns and become pono with who I am, who they are, then reconnect.

About Aloha

My daily practice and my approach to life include the deeper meanings of the word *aloha*. Even if you've never visited Hawai'i, you're probably familiar with the word. Most people think of "aloha" as a greeting, but it only became a greeting around the time the American missionaries arrived. The deeper meaning of "aloha" is taught by breaking down the word into five specific concepts.

The first A in "aloha," is *ao*. *Ao* means "the light." Earlier in this book, I told the story of being out in the dark when the motion detector set off the flood lamp. The point was that you are standing in the light and now must expand the light. I ask myself every day, "Do I connect more with my light? Do I connect more with my path?" Life is light and dark, positive and negative. We choose where to place our focus.

A also stands for *ala,* which means "to be aware." *Ala* is to be aware of your path, to be aware of what's happening around you. When you're aware, you listen. You tend to be more thoughtful with others and act more appropriately to the situation. In contrast, people without *ala* who focus only on themselves tend to be overbearing or insensitive.

L is *lokahi,* which means "oneness with others and with everything." It's feeling united with the people around you. I practice hoʻoponopono with my daughter and with my son because I want to unite with who they are becoming, to see them growing more and more into who they are.

When my daughter was born, she had to sleep in her crib by herself with the room totally blacked out. I called her my princess of the darkness. She couldn't have even a single beam of light coming into her room. It was so crazy.

Then she got really sick when she was around two. As a baby, she never wanted to sleep with Mom and Dad.

As a two-year-old, she didn't want to sleep alone. She was afraid. I remember, one night, she rolled over and grabbed me. Her lips were blue, and she said, "Daddy, I can't breathe." It was one of the scariest moments of my life.

She doesn't even remember any of this. She has no recollection of it whatsoever. Do I connect with her as that three-year-old or as a nine-year-old who wants independence and to be out on her own? Ho'oponopono allows you to reconnect with your loved ones and see them for who they are. So I don't see my girl as that five-year-old that told me, "I always want to live with you, Daddy," I see her as a beautiful young lady, growing more independent every day.

Lokahi is united. In my book *The Foundation of Huna*, I talk about uniting internally and externally. In the context of ho'oponopono, do you unite with the person who's in front of you, or do you unite with the person who you knew in the past? Do I connect with Skylar as a nine-year-old or as a two-year-old? If I connect with a two-year-old, I prevent her from growing.

The O of aloha is *oiai'o*, which means "truthful." To me, the O of aloha means "transparency," to just be you. I ended a fouteen-year relationship. If you read any of my previous books, you'll see that I dedicated one of them to my ex. I'm not going to change that unless I rewrite the entire book. She is an amazing woman.

Both of us came to the conclusion that our relationship was over. I then had to speak my truth to people, with fear that students might leave me, with fear that my kids might freak out. I had fear. If you don't speak your truth, though, the fear grows and the anger grows because it grows inside you.

When you can speak your truth, when you can share with someone in a nice way, "Here's what's going on," you feel relieved, and honestly, they do, too.

Truthfulness doesn't mean being jerk, blurting out whatever is on your mind. It means being transparent. Skylar was seven at the time, and a seven-year-old needs to hear one thing. Ethan was fourteen, and a fourteen-year-old needs to hear another thing. My students needed to hear something else. Truthfulness doesn't mean that you say things you don't want to. Truthfulness means that you're being honest.

A student came up to me in the middle of all the drama of my relationship breaking up and asked me a question. I said, "It's none of your business." That's being truthful. Being truthful doesn't mean you have to open the doors to everyone. It means that you can be honest and say, "You're not a family member. There's no reason I should tell you any of this."

The H of aloha balances truthfulness. H is *haʻahaʻa*, which is to be humble. It means that you can't walk around with an inflated ego, thinking you know everything there is to know.

In terms of forgiveness, humility also includes humbling yourself to your own path. In my book *The Foundation of Huna*, I talk about people who say, "I'm just playing the hand I was dealt." The problem is that you weren't dealt the hand. You picked the hand, the card, and the suit. Sometimes, you've got to be humble and admit, "Oh, right. I picked this path." You need to humble yourself and realize that you're just an individual. You're just who you are.

Another part of humbling yourself is to recognize that the tough things you went through, the things you're working to forgive, are in the past. Like in the book *The Little Soul and the Sun*, maybe the person who wronged you was asked to do what they did so that you'd get the lesson. Maybe you begged that person to be a jerk in your life so that you could get a deeper lesson. As long as you hold onto making that person the bad guy, you don't get the lesson, and you've made their sacrifice pointless. Humbleness is accepting—accepting who you are, accepting your path, and being pono with it.

The last A in aloha is *aho nui,* meaning "patient perseverance." Diane did ho'oponopono once, and she was over a physical assault that most of us can't even comprehend. My daughter needed to do the process multiple times to get over the loss of her best friend.

There's no rhyme or reason why forgiveness takes ten times for one person and just once for someone else. Life is not an end. Life is an aim. It is a journey. To think that you can eat one salad and be physically fit, or to think that you can release all your stuff one time and be enlightened is a total misconception.

It's a daily practice, something you do on a regular basis. I do ho'oponopono every single night before I go to sleep. It helps me to wake up every day as if it's a new sunrise and a new connection.

The final A of aloha is also *aloha*, which means "absolute true love." It's the kind of love that does not make comparisons, grade people or judge them. Aloha includes mercy, compassion, and kindness. It's pretty obvious that you can't really have aloha with people you haven't forgiven.

(To learn more about aloha, Huna, and other spiritual paths, please see the Resources Section at the end of this book.)

Summary

While on the morning news show *Good Morning Sacramento*, the host asked me if I believed in a "quick fix." To her surprise, I said, "Yes, I do." I followed up by saying, "However, it is a quick fix that you need to apply every day of your life."

Think of ho'oponopono as eating a healthy meal or working out regularly. This is for your spiritual and emotional health and well-being. And yes, it is a quick fix when you compare it to other processes or therapies out there. Think of Diane's inspirational story. Since going through ho'oponopono one time in a live event in San Diego, I have seen Diane several times over the past two years, and she is still better than ever and loving life. That was quick!

Even my daughter had a relatively fast recovery from the death of her friend. While she had to go through the release a few times, in comparison to other techniques out there, this was fast. That was years ago. Her turnaround and ability to talk about her loss with clarity and freedom of emotional baggage inspires me and motivates me to offer ho'oponopono to others.

Both Diane and my daughter now do ho'oponopono regularly. It has become a part of their regular practice. When I am asked what I do on a daily basis, this is the first thing I mention. Hopefully you are now able to see why.

Give yourself time with this. For some, it is like peeling back the layers of an onion. For others, the release is so rapid that you almost question if the release was real. The proof is always in your personal reaction and experience. Notice the change and how you have improved. And like eating a healthy meal, do it again, and again.

Mahalo Nui Loa and A Hui Hou!

Acknowledgements

I would like to take a moment to acknowledge a few people that have made this book and what I do possible.

First is my mom. She has always been a guiding force in my life and has shown me what a strong, empowered woman can do.

I would like to thank my Papa Tom. He has been the father I never had and has shown me what an empowered, caring, loving man can do.

I would like to acknowledge my Grandpa Rod for all the gentle learnings he provided me along my early path. He would have loved this book, and while he never learned any of the things that I teach, he was naturally the most forgiving person I have ever known.

I would like to thank my father for teaching me ho'oponopono. My path of teaching this work is possible because of him.

I would like to acknowledge all the teachers that have guided me directly and indirectly through the years, and specifically five of them for making this work a part of my path: Uncle George Na'ope, my spiritual mentor, teacher, and guide, I miss you so much; Kumu Etua Lopes, for being my kumu and teaching me about dedication and aho nui (patient perseverance) more than I would have ever believed possible; John Ka'imikaua, for guiding our workshops and helping to lay the foundation of this path; and Mornah Simiona and David Bray Jr., for teaching my father, who in turn taught me.

I would also like to acknowledge my fiancé, Tris Thorp, for helping me to find myself again. In you, I found my soul mate and a deep love that brought me back to my teachings.

Finally, I would like to acknowledge all my students. This book is for you, because without you, I could not be a kumu (teacher).

Mahalo to you all.

About the Author

A dedicated Master Trainer of NLP and respected expert on Ho'oponopono (Hawaiian forgiveness process), Dr. Matt James empowers students in NLP, Hypnosis, Mental Emotional Release® Therapy, and a 28-generation lineage of Huna—energy, healing and spiritual development utilized in ancient Hawai'i. Dr. Matt is certainly making his life a living demonstration of the extraordinary power of this wisdom. Along the way, he has picked up several university degrees, including an MA in organizational management and a PhD in health (integrative) psychology. He is the author of *The Foundation of Huna: Ancient Wisdom for Modern Times*, *Find Your Purpose, Master Your Path*, and *Integrate the Shadow, Master Your Path*. Dr. Matt is a regular contributor to *The Huffington Post* and *Psychology Today*. Visit www.drmatt.com and www.empowermentpartnership.com to learn more.

About the Empowerment Partnership

Dr. Matt James, president of the Empowerment Partnership, embodies the principles he teaches. While devoting himself to the integrity of his spiritual path, Dr. Matt has built an international firm dedicated to personal transformation, authored several books, and trained thousands of students every year in mastery of the four bodies of empowerment. Supported by a team of expert trainers, Dr. Matt weaves effective modern technologies with the timeless wisdom of ancient spiritual paths.

Dr. Matt began meditating at the age of five, and through his childhood learned spiritual practices directly from such teachers as Baba Muktananda. He also studied Huna, the original science of consciousness of the Hawaiian Islands, from Uncle George Na'ope who was honored as one of Hawaii's Golden Living Treasures. Dr. Matt received the gift of carrying on one of the ancient lineages of Huna, the Bray Family lineage, from Hawaiian elders.

The Empowerment Partnership is the world's foremost organization specializing in alternative and integrative approaches to psychology, human understanding, and personal growth.

Through our diverse experiences and educations, as well as cumulative years of advanced teachings, we have developed proven techniques that merge psychological and neurological sciences with ancient Hawaiian spiritual teachings to help you:

- Create instant rapport with others
- Process information and communicate in more dynamic ways
- Overcome procrastination, depression, and phobias
- Our Purpose is to Actively Empower the World

Other Books by Dr. Matt James

Find Your Purpose, Master Your Path, 2012, Advanced Neuro Dynamics, Inc.

Integrate the Shadow, Master Your Path, 2014, Balboa Press Publishing

The Foundation of Huna: Ancient Wisdom for Modern Times, 2011, Create Space Publishing

Mental and Emotional Release®, 2017 Balboa Press Publishing

Connect with the Author

Websites:
www.empowermentpartnership.com
www.drmatt.com
www.huna.com
www.nlp.com

Email: info@nlp.com

Business Address:
75-6099 Kuakini Hwy
Kailua – Kona, Hawaii 96740

Social Media:

Facebook:	https://www.facebook.com/ EmpowermentPartnership/
LinkedIn:	https://www.linkedin.com/ company-beta/10831237/
Instagram:	https://www.instagram.com/ empowermentpartnership/
YouTube:	https://www.youtube.com/user/ DrMattJames
Huffington Post:	http://www.huffingtonpost.com/ author/matt-303
Psychology Today:	https://www.psychologytoday. com/experts/matt-james-phd
Podcast:	https://itunes.apple.com/ us/podcast/empower-your- life-with-dr-matt-james/ id1135367575?mt=2

Resources

For further information and insight into Hoʻoponopono, here are some resources I think you'll find valuable:

Huna Workshop offered in Kona, Hawaiʻi
For information about the Huna Workshop, please visit Huna.com or DrMatt.com

Books/Audio Recordings available at ShopNLP.com
The Foundation of Huna, Ancient Wisdom for Modern Times
While honoring the integrity of Huna, Dr. Matt translates Huna's primordial teachings into contemporary realities, offering practical applications of Huna principles to enhance health, prosperity, and well-being in all aspects of life.

Hoʻoponopono Audio Recording
Hoʻoponopono ("to make right") is a healing process used by ancient Hawaiians of the past and those that practice Huna today to align with and clean up our genealogy, as well as to clean up our relationships with other people in our lives. When we forgive others, we forgive ourselves. This audio recording uses closed-eye guided visualizations, so please listen to it in a comfortable, relaxing, safe environment.

Blog Posts available on the topics of Huna, Hoʻoponopono, and Forgiveness
http://www.drmatt.com/nlp/huna/
https://www.psychologytoday.com/blog/focus-forgiveness
https://goo.gl/Rj9rdA
https://goo.gl/HiyVYo

YouTube Videos

https://youtu.be/g96ABh0HjGw Hoʻoponopono

https://youtu.be/uFY7Vurv5zQ Huna and Energy Explained P1

https://youtu.be/daRWefzeTtc Huna and Energy Explained P2

Membership Site with on-demand access to Dr. Matt's Huna and Hoʻoponopono Collection … Coming Soon! www.empowermentsuccess.com